DATE DUE

How To Plan and Book Meetings and Seminars
2nd Edition

How to Plan and Book Meetings and Seminars

2nd edition

by

Judy Williams

Ross Books
P. O. Box 4340,
Berkeley, CA 94704

Library of Congress Cataloging-in-Publication Data

Williams, Judy, 1949-
  How to plan and book meetings and seminars.
Includes index.
  1. Meetings—Handbooks, manuals, etc.
  2. Seminars—Handbooks, manuals, etc.
  3. Scheduling (Management) I. Title.
AS6.W53 1987 658.4'563 86-31601

ISBN 978-0-89496-055-0 (pbk.)

ISBN 978-0-89496-000-0 (eBook)

CONTENTS

Contents

Introduction

My main purpose is to educate. If, however, a smile should cross your lips from time to time as you read this, I will have also entertained you. Good ... I believe learning should be fun! It should also be quick and to the point! Who has time these days to pour over great volumes of information about any new subject? After all, in addition to your job, you might be involved with tennis lessons, football games, or perhaps you are writing The Great American Novel.

Seriously, there is no reason why so many of you are in the dark regarding the "how to" of booking a meeting at a hotel or other facility outside the office. I know that often you find yourself caught in a "seat-of-your-pants" crisis requiring immediate action on a subject you know little about.

I want to enlighten you on this subject by first

teaching you some of the lingo used by hotel personnel (a language all its own) and giving you a working knowledge of that special language. You will see that communication and follow-up will become your best friends.

Secondly, I will guide you step-by-step through a sample booking. It will involve the booking of meeting space with appropriate room set-up, sleeping accommodations, meal functions including a cocktail reception, audio-visual equipment and direct billing! Later, I will present the script of a typical telephone dialogue between you and the hotel contact.

Whenever possible, I will describe thoughts and procedures from the hotel contact's point of view and let you in on the thought process behind some of the things the hotel asks of you. No one likes to look stupid. No one likes to feel that if they had known more about a certain subject they could have asked more intelligent questions. Familiarization with this book will prevent that from happening. Sure, there will still be areas that you won't be totally familiar with, but your increased knowledge will allow you to ask questions with confidence.

Together, we will explore how to get that much-needed information from the boss; how to organize yourself; and then convey your wishes to the hotel contact.

Hopefully, after you book your next meeting, be it your first or maybe just your best, you can look back with pride at the conclusion.

You will have performed admirably in communicating what, on occasion, may seem some very bizarre requests, made decisions on your own, and followed through effectively to get the job done. (Just think, if you get real good at this, you might get to do it more often.) Your reward will be the satisfaction of a job well done.

If you're booking for your boss, you want him or her to come through all of this like a "hero" for putting on such a fine meeting. Ideally, your boss will feel as though the efforts of both of you have paid off in a very positive way.

The hotel will have put all of your requests together and seen that everything was executed correctly in a professional and friendly manner. The bottom line is a meeting that comes off without a hitch!

There is, however, no magical formula to guarantee that every meeting will be a smashing success. However, careful preparation will eliminate last minute problems. Attention to detail, follow-up, a good working relationship with your hotel contact and a lot of common sense will also help to insure that success.

I will be concentrating mainly on booking everything outside your present meeting facility. Granted, right now you may hold your meetings in your own conference room, the library at school, or in a church classroom. Some day you might need to book overnight accommodations in conjunction with those meetings. Your group may someday (often sooner than you think) outgrow that meeting room and you will be setting up meetings away from your present facility in their entirety.

You might find that the policies of your favorite hotel vary somewhat from what I have experienced. (Don't worry if you don't *have* a favorite hotel, I'll teach you how to find one.) Remember, *your* meetings should be tailored specifically to suit your needs.

You will find yourself beginning to book meetings with confidence. Confidence that will grow stronger with each meeting booked. With the help of your hotel contact you will continually improve the quality of your bookings, always keeping in mind the wishes of your boss and the comfort and satisfaction of your attendees.

You will come to learn that booking meetings can be a lot less scary than you first expected, and might even be fun as you begin to put your imagination to work!

Chapter 1

It Happens This Way: or, Who Needs This Book?

I don't know how we get ourselves into these situations, but we do. Usually when it's time to book a meeting or a banquet, it comes as a total surprise. A surprise to you anyway. It's never a good time either— it's usually when you are already behind schedule or dealing with a crisis situation at home or at work that you get hit with this! Let's look at six examples of some people who may wind up booking a meeting at a moment's notice.

Perhaps you're a **Corporate Administrative Assistant...**

"Ms. Hawthorne!" The voice came through the intercom as if from a man who had just had a revelation. "I want to have a meeting!" Your boss seemed to scream with enthusiasm.

"Good Lord, not at five o'clock!" you think to yourself.

"I want to have it next month. Get all our reps in here, spend a couple of nights, set up some lunches. Let's do it the first part of the month. I'll be out of town the first of next week . . . get together with you after that."

"Yes Sir!" — Yes Sir? You wonder what you've agreed to! The closest thing to a meeting you've ever booked was four people in your own conference room. They came *in* for the day and went *out* to lunch. Now we're talking about meeting space, meals, sleeping accommodations, transportation, all the details, all the responsibility. Where do you begin?

Or, maybe you're an **Association Secretary . . .**

"Now, Mrs. Mitchell, we'll need a luncheon set up for about fifteen people. Just our officers and a few administrative personnel from the school. How about Saturday, the ninth? Can you see to that?" Mrs. Johnson inquired.

"Sure I can," you replied. "Same place as usual?"

"No, let's look at another location. The service has not been up to par lately at our usual meeting place. Check around, see what you can come up with." She answered.

You had never booked a group luncheon before you became secretary of the PTA at your son's school. This duty comes with the territory and you're obliged to handle it. You've been using the same hotel and banquet facility that Dr. Kramer, your predecessor, had used, but now Mrs. Johnson wants to change all that.

You wonder where to start.
Or, maybe you're a **Regional Manager of a Cosmetics Firm . . .**

You know that sales have been down. You need to get everyone together to boost morale, but at the same time take care of some serious business. As you lean back in your chair, the plan begins to come together.

"Suppose I book a meeting at one of the nearby resort locations and set up some recreational activities as well. Maybe then I could get through to my employees that I appreciate what they have done for me, but we still need to work hard to pull out of this slump. It just might be the boost we need!"

"Better still, I'll set it up on a weekend and they can bring their spouses or a guest. Let's see now, that would be about a hundred and fifty people . . . weekend meetings interspersed with recreational activities. I'll need to book meeting space, meals, rooms, maybe tennis or golf—but I've never done this before . . ."

Or, maybe you're an **Entrepreneur . . .**

"You really are a dynamic public speaker, Ray. You ought to form your own company and do motivational seminars. There are millions of people out there who would benefit from your enthusiasm and vitality."

Thinking back, those had been the words of a trusted friend and, at the time, a fellow employee. Now, six months later, you had taken her advice.

You are now the president of your own company and embarking on a trail of motivational seminars designed to inspire the most timid of men and women. You need to book good locations with great service and reasonable prices. You have an idea of what you need because you've attended numerous seminars of this sort. You need a hotel meeting room with theatre style seating for three hundred or so. Meals and sleeping accommodations will be the responsibility of the participants. You'll speak in various cities across the country. But where do you begin?

Or, perhaps you're a member of an **Arts Group** . . .

"We need recognition. We need to have our work seen by the general public." Frank Howell said as he put down his paintbrush.

"That's right, how are we ever going to sell our work if no one knows about it?" Becky Wilson inquired as she stopped to get more clay from the bin.

"We're all good craftsmen." Frank continued. "We enjoy what we do and it shows in our work. We just need a boost, someplace where we can display our artwork . . . maybe a show . . . That's it! We'll organize a show!" His enthusiasm for this new project was clear. "But which of us knows how to plan and book an Arts and Crafts show? We'll need exhibition space, notification letters, an ad in the local papers, a chairperson. What do we do first?"

Or, you could be a **Travel Agent** . . .

"Did you confirm Alex Masters' airline reservation?" June Dozier, the manager of the travel agency, asked.

"Yes, he is confirmed on the 10:00 A.M. flight tomorrow." You answered. You also wondered why June had bothered to ask. She knew you were careful with your work and that you had seldom, if ever, neglected to change an airline or hotel reservation when asked to do so. Something else seemed on her mind.

"Can you come into my office for a moment?" She was heading that way as she spoke.

"Sure, be right there." You didn't have time to won der if you had done something wrong, just grabbed your note pad and pen and followed her through the door.

"Shut the door, would ya'?" June gestured toward the door.

"This has got to be bad news," you thought as you sat down across from her.

"I need your help." she began, "Alex Masters' account is very important to us. For a long time now, he has used this agency exclusively to book his airline flights, his hotel rooms, and even his family vacations each year. I had lunch with him yesterday. Seems his business is growing by leaps and bounds and he wants to start having monthly meetings with all his reps. He has, oh/twenty-five to thirty reps in various locations. This could mean a lot of business for us. The catch is this: He wants us to book the entire meeting for him. Wants it set up at a local hotel, rooms blocked, meals planned, everything! And of course, there will still be airline arrangements to be made. He understands that we don't have a Corporate Meeting Planning Division per se, but he'd like us to handle it if we think we can. I'd like you to be in charge of this and I think you can do it. What do you think?"

You were conscious only of the fact that your head was nodding affirmatively. Meanwhile, the thoughts racing through your mind all culminated at one important fact: You needed a quick course in booking meetings. You wondered if there was a book on the subject . . .

You probably found yourself fitting, at least in part, into one of these examples. It can all be very over-whelming and taking that first step isn't easy.

Usually you begin with very little information; information that is, at best, vague, general, ambiguous, and likely to change at any time. Fear of the unknown will also do its part to intimidate you. If you feel like you *can't* do it, it's only because you've never done it before, or not on this large a scale. I say you *can* do it. And very well at that!

Let's begin slowly. We'll look at the key players involved and examine what each must do to ensure the meeting's success.

Chapter 2

The Key Players and Their Roles

Who Are the Key Players?

There are three major players in this game. They are:

1. The Instigator (the person who decides to hold the meeting)
2. The Coordinator (you)
3. The Hotel Contact

For convenience' sake, we'll call the instigator "the boss," because that's who it usually is. Of course, if you're booking your own meeting, then you're the instigator as well as the coordinator, and you have double the responsibility. (Look on the bright side,

at least you have only half the communication problems!)

Mix-ups of any kind will generally be the responsibility, directly or indirectly, of one or more of these
key people,

Two Elements of Success

There are two thoughts to keep in mind. If you
will remember these words of wisdom you will have
greater success and a better working relationship all
around.

Communication is essential
Follow-up makes it work

communicate
follow-up

*Watch for these words in the outside margins of this
book. They'll serve as reminders when it's particularly
important, or essential, to the success of your meeting that
you* communicate *and/or* follow-up. *Used properly they
make an unbeatable combination. The key players should
make every effort to communicate and follow-up time and
again.*

Each of these key people also have his or her own
responsibilities to this meeting. They must all understand their responsibilities and know that if anyone
falters, the entire efforts of the others will suffer. The
players must support each other.

Responsibilities of the Instigator

The instigator, or boss, is directly responsible for
providing all information needed to book this meeting. This is true. Read it again. I said "providing all
information." Now, granted, he may delegate to you
the authority to make some of the decisions. Ulti-
mately, however, he must guide you in achieving his

goals. It may only mean telling you what he wants (now that shouldn't be too difficult . . .).

But, if he doesn't have his plans formulated, there is no way you can book this meeting. I don't mean that he needs to know exactly what he is going to say to his attendees, but he must tell you dates, times, who is to be invited, his preferred seating arrangements, audiovisual equipment needs, food and beverage requirements and types of sleeping accommodations. (And remember—Once he has communicated you can bet that he will follow-up.) Now I hope his giving you this information doesn't seem like a lot to ask. Every one of these categories involves a monumental amount of work for you and the conference manager. Once you have this information you can proceed. The sum of your success will greatly depend however, upon the amount and quality of information you received from the boss in the beginning. The boss must also be reasonably available to you to answer any quick questions that were not addressed initially for one reason or another.

I cannot stress strongly enough the simple fact that your boss must tell you what she wants. She *communicate* must communicate. It will be up to you to convince your boss that the success of her meeting is directly related to the quantity and quality of the information she shares with you. If necessary, make an appointment to discuss the meeting requirements with her. Be persistent, but be professional. You must also be prepared to discuss these requirements intelligently. Once she sees that her cooperation up front, in the beginning stages of all this, is the key to smooth sailing right on through the actual meeting itself, she will be eager to share information with you. I honestly believe that your professional attitude and enthusiasm will inspire her to work with you, no matter how busy she is.

Responsibilities of the Coordinator

Your obligations will be to effectively communicate meeting requirements, all inclusive, between your boss and the hotel contact. That means every detail that relates to any part of the meeting. On many occasions you will assume the responsibilities of your boss and make decisions for him. This will come naturally as you become more familiar with your particular company's typical requirements.

I can assure you, however, that "crystal balls" are no longer "standard equipment" for hotel Conference Managers. They have no way of knowing what you want unless you tell them.

communicate
follow-up

Additionally, your responsibilities will encompass the communication to your attendees of the details of the meeting and the follow-up associated with it. In your notification letter, you will inform your attendees of the date and location of the meeting. You will also advise them to let you know, by a certain date, if they need overnight accommodations. You'll find detailed information on this in Chapter 15.

You may also be involved in making arrangements to transport some attendees to and from an airport or train station, possibly scheduling a "tour of the plant", or become the entertainment director for the spouses who might be coming along. More on this in Chapter 12.

You are probably getting the message that you will do a variety of jobs in conjunction with this meeting. You will be the key to keeping the channel of communication open.

Responsibilities of the Hotel Contact

The Hotel Contact's responsibility to you is to execute your contractual specifications to the letter.

He/She will be your liaison between the various departments within the hotel:

1. General Manager: company policies
2. Front Desk Manager: all check-in, check-out and posting procedures
3. Food and Beverage Director: all food and beverage functions
4. Banquet Coordinator: all setup and serving personnel
5. Housekeeping Department: all sleeping room needs
6. Maintenance Engineer: air conditioning/heating and lighting comfort
7. Controller: your charges and getting them paid.
8. Sales: coordination and execution of all meeting and banquet functions

It will be your contact's job to communicate your wishes to these departments and then follow-up to see that they are carried out. *communicate follow-up*

Additions, deletions, changes of any kind to the original signed agreement, whether these changes are in writing or handled by a telephone conversation, will also be the responsibility of a caring, reputable hotel who values your continued business. (I hope you are not giving your meeting business to any other kind.)

Many times as Conference Manager I looked into my "crystal ball" for guidance. (We still had them back then . . .) At first, it seemed to me that bosses and their assistants really didn't care if their meetings went well or not. They could, after all, always blame the hotel if anything went wrong. This was, of course, not usually the case. I saw as time went by that generally the secretaries just weren't knowledgeable about meeting planning. They didn't really understand what I needed from them to carry out their wishes. So, individually, I would guide them carefully through their booking, explaining, as time permitted, why I needed certain information.

I also tried to anticipate problems before they arose. I checked every meeting room before the boss/instructor ever stepped foot into it, checked coffee breaks well ahead of their arrival time, inspected meal room set ups, and double checked with the chef on meal preparation and timing.

Playing devil's advocate and trying to stay one step ahead of everyone and everything drove many of my associates crazy! But I got my fair share of "Happy Letters" and business certainly didn't suffer because of it. Even so, I was told once (by an uncaring management person) that the job of conference manager could be done by anyone. I suppose it can. It is how WELL it is done that is important.

Do bear in mind that your contact at a hotel may not be as conscientious or may be even more so. It may be any one of a number of fully qualified persons. Titles will vary from hotel to hotel depending on the size of the operation or company policy regarding job descriptions and respective titles. You might book your meeting with a Sales Secretary, Sales Representative, Sales Manager, Banquet Coordinator, Conference Manager, Catering Manager, Director of Sales or even a General Manager! Your concern should not be with titles but more with their performance and understanding of your needs.

Now that we have a good idea of who is responsible for what, let's look at the information you need to be familiar with.

Chapter 3

Dates and Times

When you call the hotel, the first thing you will tell your contact is the date you want to have your meeting.

Checking Dates

The hotel has a *function book*. This book is used to keep track of all of the companies or individuals who book with them. When you call and request a certain date they will determine availability by consulting this book. If appropriate space is available, based on the number of attendees and style of seating you request, the hotel will *block* or *reserve* it in your company name.

Definite and Tentative Dates

Meeting space may be blocked on a definite or tentative basis.

A definite booking is just that—definite. You are sure you are having a meeting and you are sure you want to meet at that particular hotel. Check with your hotel contact regarding their cancellation policy. On occasion, you may need to block space on a tentative basis.

For example, if the home office should call and say that a meeting will occur in your region, but gives you little more than the date and number of attendees, you will probably want to call the hotel and reserve space on a tentative basis. Chances are good that the hotel will inquire as to when you will be able to make this definite and give them further details. (Save yourself a phone call. When you are talking to the home office, ask them when they think they will have further information for you.)

Remember, if the hotel should receive a request for a definite booking that requires space that they are holding for you on a tentative basis, you may be called and given twenty-four hours to make it definite or relinquish the space. If you book space on a tentative basis be sure to ask the hotel what their policy is. Tentative bookings are the exception and not the rule.

Inclusive Dates

When you call to book your meeting be sure to include all dates your group will occupy the meeting room. Do not say "I need a meeting room the first week of June." You will have to be specific. For instance, you might say "I need a meeting room from 9:00 A.M. to 5:00 P.M. on Monday, June 3rd and Tuesday, June 4th. I will require classroom seating for 25 to 30 attendees and a lunch in a separate room each day." At that point, the hotel contact should refer to the function book to determine availability. No sense in getting further into details of the meeting if space is not available.

Be sure to discuss any day or part of a day, before or after the actual meeting dates, that your boss or instructor might need access to that meeting room. Do not assume (that is a no-no word) that she will be able to set-up her posters, lay out her materials and run through her presentation the night before. (Your boss or instructor may find herself sitting on a box outside the meeting room waiting for the local Woman's Club meeting to adjourn!)

If the hotel will be setting up the room the evening before the start of your meeting, they may allow your boss/instructor to use the room (after a certain hour) to set up her materials. If your boss needs the room for a portion (or better part of) a day, there may be an additional charge involved in order to reserve the room for that period of time. At any rate, communicate your exact requirements and discuss any additional charges. Follow-up by making sure these details are on the written contract.

communicate

follow-up

Unavailable Dates

If you find that appropriate space is not available on the dates you have requested and you want to stay with this particular hotel, consider alternate available meeting dates. Discuss these with your boss and get back with the hotel as soon as possible.

In the event that you cannot change your dates, you will need to contact another hotel to check on availability.

Starting and Ending Times

In addition to your dates, you will need to know certain times. Be as specific as possible about starting and ending times each day. Most hotels will require specific times and rigid adherence to those times. A meeting that runs later than the agreed time becomes a real worry for the conference manager as well as set up personnel and, if they are aware of the delay, the next group to use the room! Be sure your boss gives you true starting and ending times and that she plans to abide by them. Otherwise, she may open herself up to severe chastisement by hotel personnel, often not in the most discreet manner.

If the starting and ending times vary on a multiple day meeting, be sure to call that to the attention of your contact.

For example, on the first day of your meeting you may actually begin at noon. You would probably have the room all day (and be charged accordingly). One of the reasons, however, for letting the hotel know your exact starting time is so that the hotel banquet staff may bring freshly iced water into the meeting room ten to fifteen minutes prior to the actual start of the meeting. (You see, when you are asked for exact starting times it really isn't a conspiracy to make your life miserable, it may be a genuine effort to pinpoint the "ice-water-arrival-time".)

By the same token, if you will conclude early on a specific day, letting the hotel know will allow them to schedule their banquet set-up personnel to either freshen your room for tomorrow's meeting or break it down and reset it for the next group coming in.

Twenty-four Hour Bookings

One more word of caution: If you book a meeting room for more than one day and will have let's say, the same room set-up, be sure to inquire about whether you will have the room on a twenty-four hour basis. Otherwise, you could find that the room will be cleared and reset (because it has been rented to someone else in the evening) and set again according to your specifications for your meeting in the morning. This would mean that someone connected with your meeting might have to go back in prior to your meeting the next day and lay out the materials and reset displays, literature, etc. (Try to avoid this if at all possible.)

This situation could also arise if your hotel is unable to book your meeting in the same room for all of the days. You should be told this at the time of the booking and it should also appear on the written agreement from the hotel.

follow-up

communicate

If you find this arrangement very inconvenient, tell the hotel contact. They might be able to move a group or, in the event of a cancellation, you will at least have first consideration. Remember—if you have a very elaborate audio-visual presentation, it may not be practical for your meeting room location to be changed once the meeting has begun. You might have to book your meeting elsewhere in order to insure continual use of the same room.

Break Time

Times for breaks and meal functions should be specified at this time. If you are unsure of exact times for breaks and meal functions give your contact a rough idea when they might be. More specific times can be called in after you and your boss finalize the *follow-up*   agenda. Make a note to follow-up.

As a rule, morning breaks are generally around 10:00 or 10:30. Afternoon breaks should be about half-way between lunch and the end of the meeting. Lunch may be scheduled to begin anywhere from 12:00 to 1:00 depending on how late the meeting is scheduled to begin. One hour is generally the duration of a lunch period.

It will be helpful to indicate when the attendees will return to the meeting room after lunch. While your attendees are eating (either on their own or at a group meal in another room), the banquet set-up personnel, or "housemen" as they are often called, should be freshening the meeting room. They should empty trash cans and ashtrays, straighten all chairs and freshen water stations. If no afternoon break is planned, they will remove the break table or at least all perishable parts of it. (Uneaten danish, cream pitchers, leftover stale coffee, warm orange juice . . .)

As a rule, housemen will not move any personal items. Usually, they will not straighten or rearrange any papers on the tables. It is always a good idea, however, to inform your attendees that the room will be straightened during the lunch break (if the hotel is in fact going to do this. Don't end up with egg on your face, or your boss'. It may not be the policy of the hotel to straighten during lunch breaks). Of course, it goes without saying that women should take their purses with them to lunch (common sense here, but you never know . . .).

Chapter 4

The Necessary Numbers

Your hotel contact was able to check availability of meeting space because in addition to meeting dates and times, you provided an estimate of the number of attendees.

How Your Estimate Is Used

On occasion, someone would actually call the hotel wanting to know if I had space available for a meeting but without knowing how many people would be attending!

Get as close as possible on your estimate of attendees. The hotel contact will use this number to determine the size of room you will need based upon your specific seating arrangements. They will then determine if the appropriate meeting room is available on the dates you have requested.

Why You Must Be Accurate

Errors in estimating your number of attendees can be devastating. If your estimate is too high, your group may end up being in a room two or three times too large. (How does your boss look behind a bullhorn?) An estimate that is too low might, in reality, grow so large that your attendees would feel like sardines. The hotel might even be unable to accommodate your group due to this increase. So you see, a close-as-you-can-come estimate of attendees is vital from the very beginning.

Generally, you will quote a range of attendees. For example, if you add up the number of people you think will attend and it comes to eleven or twelve, tell the hotel you will need a room that will accommodate ten to fifteen persons. Similarly, if your estimate comes to seventy-five, a quote of seventy-five to one hundred will be acceptable. An irresponsible quote of "twenty-five to one hundred" will definitely alert the hotel that you do not know what you are doing!

Tips on Arriving at Your Estimate

Base your estimate somewhere between what you feel is a minimum possible attendance and a maximum possible attendance. The somewhere-between number allows for last minute "nays" that become "yeas", illnesses, prior commitments and outright lies.

There are a couple of things that will help you determine how many participants to expect:

1. Look at whether it is a mandatory meeting. (Those

are easy—The only acceptable excuse for absence is that they have to go to their own funeral! Which is where they will be going if they don't show up at this meeting!)
2. Consider actual attendance figures from previous meetings similar to this one.
3. The boss is one of your best sources for determining the number of attendees. Be sure he is in agreement with the number you decide to quote to the hotel.

If Your Numbers Change

Notify the hotel immediately of any changes in your original estimate. A change of just a few persons either way might make the room inappropriate. After the initial room assignment, based on your estimate, the hotel is really not under any obligation to accommodate you comfortably if your numbers increase or decrease drastically. They will, of course, make every effort humanly possible to do so, but on occasion it just may not be possible. You will then be looking at finding another hotel, and starting all over with a lot less lead time.

Chapter 5

Musical Chairs

Don't let words like theatre, classroom, conference, u-shape, hollow square, rounds, banquet, or reception throw you for a loop! These are merely terms for the eight most commonly used types of seating arrangements.

In this chapter, we will discuss each one in detail. Study the diagrams and descriptions carefully. Do this before you discuss seating arrangements with the boss. You might even be able to assist her in determining the best arrangement for her meeting.

Flexibility in Your Set-Up

You will need to communicate to the hotel the exact arrangement you will need. You might discover that *communicate* you need to make a few changes to the usual set-up as described in the Appendix. Feel free to do so. Bear in mind, however, that hotel housemen are trained in the basic set-ups as you see them in the diagrams. Any deviations can open the door for mistakes. I suggest that you routinely furnish the hotel with a detailed diagram clearly depicting what you want. This will help to eliminate errors due to misunderstandings.

Meeting Room Charges

Another area where you don't want any misunderstandings is in meeting room charges. These charges are influenced by many things.

1. The size of the room and the type of set-up required.
2. The amount of labor involved.
3. The amount of overhead, that is, lighting, heating and/or air conditioning costs.
4. Whether or not you are willing to pay it!

Negotiating Rates

nunicate

ollow-up

Meeting room charges may be as variable as the rooms themselves. Policy varies from hotel to hotel. It is probably the one area where the most negotiation takes place. Ask if you are being charged for the meeting room. If not, be sure it is so stipulated on the contract. Generally, you will not be charged for rooms where full meal functions are held.

Meeting room charges may vary from "no charge" to a fee of thousands of dollars. Expect higher rates in larger metropolitan cities, resort areas or peak seasons. Hotels within a certain area though should be fairly competitive. (A meeting room charge of $1,000 at a hotel in Bushy-head, Oklahoma would certainly be suspect.)

Some hotels have rigid meeting room rates, but there will be some who can be negotiated with. If it looks like your meeting will generate a lot of revenue for the hotel or perhaps the number of meetings your organization will host throughout the year could add up to substantial business, discuss a "break" on the meeting room charge.   *communicate*

Hotels will look at the total picture when making a decision on meeting room rental. They will consider revenue from sleeping rooms, planned food and beverage functions, profit from audio-visual equipment rental, incidental income from your attendees, future bookings and referrals from your company. A reduction or complete removal might be possible. In many cases, your contact will need to get permission from a superior for a reduction or removal and get back with you.

Group Sizes Defined

It is important that you become familiar with common styles of set-up and group sizes. I will suggest a range of group size for each type of set-up that follows. These suggestions are not carved in stone. They are meant as guidelines only. They are offered to prevent you from asking for "U-shape for ninety-five people", or, in the event your hotel contact suggests "banquet style for thirteen people", alerting you to say "No ... I think U-shape or three rounds of five each would be more appropriate ..." These suggestions are also based on the fact that your entire group must be accommodated in the same room at the same time. Learn these basic group sizes:

1. The small group: 2 to 25 persons

2. The medium group: 25 to 100 persons
3. The large group: 100 to 500 persons
4. The very large group: 500 on up into the 1000's.

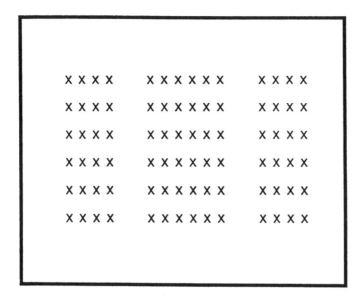

Theatre

Seats medium to large groups

This term applies to a set-up using only chairs. They will be lined up in succeeding rows, one after the other. There should be aisles on each side, one in the middle, ample room in the front for the speaker and/or presentation, and some room in the back which will allow easy access. (This is much like you would find in a movie theatre, or auditorium, thus the name "theatre".) You will probably want to request a small table up front for the instructor. Have iced water available on that table and water stations around the room for your participants. Your instructor will also need a podium and microphone with this set-up.

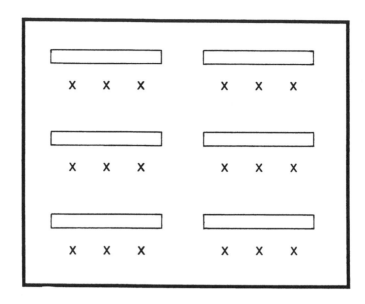

Classroom or Schoolroom

Seats virtually any size of meeting from medium to very large, space permitting

This term applies to a set-up that will use chairs and tables. The tables used are generally "narrow" classroom tables. These are approximately eighteen inches wide and six or eight feet long. The hotel will generally set three people at a six foot table and four people at an eight foot table. This will afford about two feet per person at the table. The hotel may also use "wide" tables that are approximately thirty inches wide and the same six or eight feet in length. The tables may be set to face forward in straight rows, or be placed at an angle giving your attendees a better view of the instructor and/or presentation. This angular arrangement is sometimes called "herringbone," a term derived from the shape of the spine of the herring fish. There should be ample room in the front and back with sufficient aisles for ease of movement.

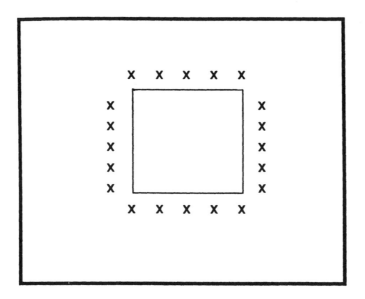

Conference

Seats smaller groups in which all participants will need to be seen and heard

A conference set-up consists of one table or a group of tables put together to form a large square or perhaps a rectangle. All participants will face the center of the table and will be equally spaced around the perimeter unless you ask for something different. This is usually the set-up you'll find in your own conference or board room.

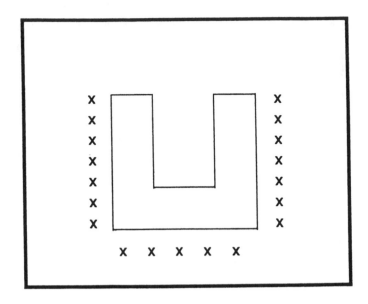

U-Shape

Seats small to medium groups up to 50 people

This set-up derives its name from (you guessed it) its shape. Very simply, it will be tables placed in the shape of a "U". Again, narrow or wide tables may be used. One end will be open and one closed. You may want to designate one end or the other as the "head," meaning the area from which the boss/ instructor will speak. Seating may be on the outside of the tables only (this is preferable) or outside and inside. This is a versatile set-up and may be used for meal functions as well.

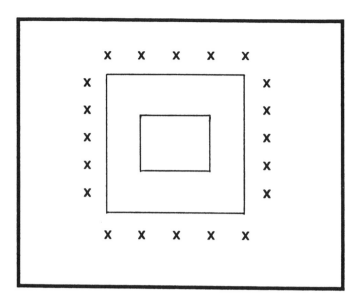

Hollow Square

Seats groups in the small to mid-size range, up to 50 people

This set-up is, as it sounds, in the shape of a square with a hole in the middle. Personally, this set-up does absolutely nothing for me, but then it may be your boss[7] favorite. Seating will be on the outside only (quite simply because you can't get into the middle!). I guess this arrangement would work well for the "unveiling" of a scale model of a shopping center or skyscraper. You may not want your attendees to have access to the model but want them to have a clear view of it.

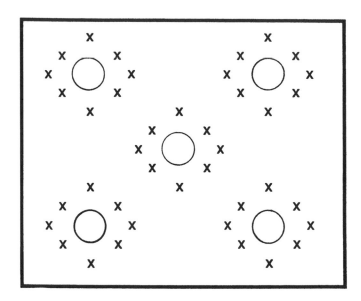

Rounds

Seats medium to very large groups

This refers to a grouping of round tables. The Rounds set-up is generally used for meal functions. If the hotel uses tables that are seventy-two inches in diameter they should seat eight to ten people comfortably (eight of course, more comfortably than ten). These tables will be placed within the room allowing ample space for servers to move about the room between them. Breakfasts, lunches or dinners may all be well served by this arrangement. Occasionally, these tables may be used for study groups or breakouts in conjunction with another style of meeting set-up.

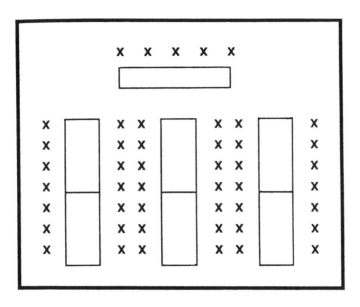

Banquet

Seats large to very large groups

Does a picture come to mind of royal feasts with gladiators, ladies-in-waiting and lots of messy, greasy food? Or did you immediately think of the football banquet you attended last year when your son was voted "Most Valuable Player"? The seating arrangements may very well have something in common.

The set-up consists of the placement of tables end-to-end in long rows throughout the room. Seating will be on both sides of the table. There should be aisles wide enough to permit servers to move easily about the room. You will often need a head table with this arrangement. (Head tables are discussed in the next chapter.)

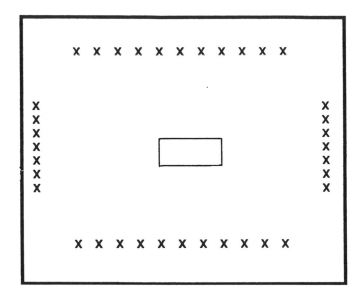

Reception

Accommodates virtually any group over 20, dependent on room size

This set-up consists chairs placed side-by-side around the perimeter of the room. It is used for stand up affairs where mingling is encouraged. The number of chairs will be kept to a minimum, usually just enough to line the room. Tables for hors d'oeuvres, desserts, coffee service, or gifts should be placed conveniently throughout the room. Be sure these additional table requirements and their placement are understood and on the contract.

This concludes our discussion on the basic types of seating arrangements. To complete the set-up and add the comforts of home, you'll need to be familiar with a few more things.

Chapter 6

Standard Expectations and Additions

How elaborately your meeting room is set up will vary from hotel to hotel. You should, however, expect a few things to be standard.

Some Things Go Without Saying, or Do They?

All tables, whether for meeting or eating, are to be covered with cloths of appropriate size. The cloths should be clean, wrinkle-free and should not have any torn places or cigarette burns. They should be placed neatly on the tables.

Seating arrangements that have seating on one

side only should be "draped long" in the front or "skirted" to create a "modesty panel". Most hotels have pre-gathered or pre-pleated skirting that they use. It too should be clean, neatly pressed and free of holes or tears.

Additional tables and accessories will sometimes be necessary to complete the set-ups we discussed in the last chapter. You will have to decide which of these you want to add to your basic set-up.

Seating Your Special Guests

A head table is set apart from the other tables, usually in the center front of the room. In a meeting environment they may accommodate one person, the instructor. In a banquet setting, up to ten, twelve or even more, where you might choose to seat the officers of a company or club, the guest speaker, the Mayor, the Governor, or even the President! These tables should always be covered with cloths and skirted.

Head tables can be placed on "risers" allowing a better view of those special persons above the rest of the group. You should tell your hotel contact if you would like your head table elevated or raised.

Risers are like pieces of stage. They are generally in sections that measure four feet by eight feet or four feet by four feet. These pieces are placed in the area where your head table will go. They are put together to form a large enough foundation for the size head table you have requested. Risers are not very high off the ground, usually twelve or eighteen inches is the extent of the elevation. They will most likely be covered with tile or carpeting. You might even use a two-tiered head table with the table in front on floor level and the one behind on risers.

Additional Tables

Registration tables can be set up inside or outside the meeting/eating room. These tables are to be covered and skirted. You will need to inform the hotel of the size, location and number of registration tables you will need. Make sure you order enough registration tables so that your guests are not kept waiting in long lines.

Audio-visual tables are additional tables or carts that will need to be placed in the meeting room from which all projectors will be operated. This usually goes without saying, but be sure to include these tables on the diagram you furnish the hotel.

communicate

Break tables are to be covered and skirted. They can be placed inside or outside the meeting room in convenient locations. If inside, they should be well out of the way of the meeting set-up. Generally, breaks are set up inside the meeting room along a back or side wall. This will eliminate the fear of someone (other than your attendees) eating or drinking from your break table. I have never seen this happen, but I guess there is always that possibility.

Display tables might be needed to display gifts, trophies, or additional information relating to the meeting. These tables should all be covered and skirted. If you have no specific request for where you would like them placed the hotel will use their discretion.

Be sure to discuss the need for these tables at the time you book your meeting. These tables are extras, not usually put into a room unless requested and not something you want thrown into the meeting room at the last minute. They should appear on the contract.

Special Touches

Water and glasses are to be placed on the meeting tables. Water should be iced and in an attractive pitcher. Pitchers should be placed every four persons or so. Glasses should be made of glass—no plastic or paper. Even the most economical hotel chain should be using glass in their meetings. All glassware is to be clean and spot free.

Ashtrays and matches are sometimes placed on the tables. If the purpose of this meeting is to discuss "The Relationship of Cigarette Smoking to Lung Cancer", for God's sake, communicate this to the hotel. They have no way of knowing what the subject of your meeting is unless you tell them. In this case, make sure that ashtrays and matches will not be placed on the tables.

If, on the other hand, you are allowing a smoking section to be established in your meeting room, inform your hotel contact where you would like it to be.

Note pads, pencils and mints are optional items that the hotel may furnish at no extra charge. They are generally not full letter or legal size pads. If you require either of these sizes, be sure to ask your contact. They will probably be glad to furnish the size you need, but at a certain cost to you.

You might want to make arrangements for **floral centerpieces** at your meal functions. Some hotels have very nice silk or dried arrangements that they use routinely. Be sure to discuss what they might have before plunging into any added expense. If they have nothing, and your meeting is a local one, you might want to make the arrangements yourself with a local florist. Be sure to advise the hotel of the arrival time of the center-pieces, and if the room will not be set up at that time, arrange for temporary cold storage (in a refrigerator, not a freezer). The best approach is to coordinate the florist to arrive after the room is set up. They can then go right into the banquet room and place each centerpiece on its appropriate table.

If you are not booking this meeting locally, beware of the hotel making the arrangements. Count on a hefty surcharge for their efforts. Again, get a price for this (including their surcharge) and make sure it appears on the contract.

You may arrange for **special occasion cakes** in the same manner as your centerpieces. If you have, for instance, a birthday in the group inquire if the hotel can arrange to have a birthday cake presented at lunchtime. They may have anything from small complimentary cakes to large, very elaborate, expensive cakes. They might have a local bakery who can come up with a personalized one at a reasonable price. Tell the hotel what you want and how much you are willing to spend. They can guide you from there.

Chapter 7

Sound and Pictures

A meeting without some audio-visual enhancement can be a dull one indeed.

Audio-visual requirements may be as simple as a flip chart or as elaborate as rear-screen projection requiring countless projectors, sound equipment, and tons of meeting space.

Audio-Visual Equipment Charges

Tell your hotel contact all of the equipment that you will need. Ask about the charges of each one. *communicate* You cannot afford any surprises in this area! There should be some things (usually not many) that you are not charged for. Perhaps a chalkboard and eraser, a podium, a screen, or maybe a stand that you will display posters on. Remember: When the hotel has to rent an item for you, the cost of rental, plus an amount added for their part in ordering and following up on the equipment, plus any delivery and pick up charges will be passed on to you. This is standard operating procedure.

A projector that you might obtain for $20 per day (you have to pick it up and take it back) might run $35 to $50 per day if the hotel makes the arrangements. It may be worth the extra cost on many occasions to free you or your boss of the responsibility. If you are booking a meeting out of town you will nearly always be at the mercy of the hotel when it comes to A.V. equipment. Be sure all equipment charges are clearly understood and in writing.

follow-up

If your boss would like to bring some equipment from the office, discuss this with the hotel contact. Generally, they will have no objections.

Let's look at the various items that fall into the audiovisual category. I will not attempt to go into detail on how each item works, but will discuss each one briefly to give you an idea of what it looks like and how it is used.

The Three Little Projectors

The most commonly used projectors are the over-head, 16mm *(sound or silent), and* carousel slide.

An overhead projector requires the use of transparencies. These are transparent pieces of celluloid on which you can draw graphs, designs, or just words and project them onto a screen by passing light through them. Most instructors bring completed transparencies with them to the meeting. Don't count on the hotel having transparencies for your boss/instructor to use at a moment's notice.

A 16mm projector is the most common one used. Your boss or instructor will furnish the film to be shown on it. A take-up reel will come with the projector. Threading and rewinding instructions are generally printed on the projector itself.

A carousel slide projector is often used as a visual aid. This projector uses a revolving tray containing slides that are projected onto the screen. Generally, the projector will have an empty tray that can be filled with individual slides your boss/instructor brings with her or just exchanged completely with an already filled tray.

A cassette slide synchronizer can be used to coordinate sound and pictures.

A Note on Rear Screen Projection

Rear screen projection is becoming more widely used. This is a procedure whereby the images are projected onto the screen from behind it. The technology is somewhat involved, but there are some things you should be aware of.

Rear screen projection requires that the screen be set twenty to twenty-five feet out into the room. Tables will be stacked up behind the screen and projectors will be placed on them. Operators will run the projectors from this backstage area. You will need to make arrangements for a curtain or draping to be placed above and on either side of the screen. Then there will need to be a six to eight foot area in front of the screen before the seating arrangement can begin.

As you can see, you must be very careful with meeting space when this kind of projection is used. Be careful also in relying on the hotel contact to arrange for necessary equipment. A reputable audio-visual company should be retained by you or the hotel to come out and do the set-up. Be careful to reserve the meeting room for ample time prior to the actual meeting. This can

communicate be a very time-consuming set-up. It is particularly
follow-up important to communicate and follow-up if you have
this type of projection.

It is not uncommon for a variety of projectors to
be used in the same meeting. Discuss projectors with
the boss and do not hesitate to ask questions about
anything you are unsure of.

In addition to projectors, there are some other
special items you will be dealing with in conjunction with the meeting. These items are flip charts,
screens, podiums, microphones *and* sound systems,
and blackboards.

Flip Charts, Screens and Podiums

A flip chart is a large pad of white paper attached
to a stand. The stand will generally be free standing
(three or four legged style) and the pad will be attached
at the top of the stand to allow clear viewing of it. Your
boss may write on it prior to or during the meeting by
using a broad tip marking pen. (Be sure to order one
when you order a flip chart.) It derives its name from
the fact that as pages are written on they may be flipped
over to the back side of the stand. This exposes the next
page available for writing. In the course of the meeting, pages may be flipped back and forth as needed.
Charges for flip charts may vary greatly. The charge
is necessitated mainly by the cost of the pad of paper.
Be sure you understand the charges when ordering a
flip chart. Some may run as high as twenty dollars per
flip chart per day. Stands, on the other hand, may be
obtained free of charge for displaying posters or pic-
communicate tures. Communicate exactly what you want.

When you order a projector, don't forget the **screen.**
(They're sort of lost without each other . . .) Screens
may or may not be a complimentary item and they

might be portable and freestanding, or built-in. Make sure the word "screen" (and any particular requests for a certain size) gets on the contract to alert set-up personnel. *follow-up*

A **podium or lectern** is a raised platform behind which a speaker stands and speaks. It may be a standing podium. This is a freestanding unit placed in front of and facing the attendees. Your boss may prefer a table-top unit. This will be placed on top of the table in an area designated as the "head" of the table. Podiums can have built in microphones and amplification or they may be no more than a basic wooden platform. The size of your meeting room and the number of attendees your boss will be speaking to will determine whether you need a microphone and amplification. A board room, for instance, with a meeting of six to fifteen people will not need amplification of any kind. A person's normal speaking voice will carry easily to those people without any help. If your boss will be speaking to a group of 50 to 100 people her voice will most probably require additional amplification. Discuss any charges for using podiums. They might be free of charge. If, however, the hotel has to rent a podium for your use, you can be sure the cost will be passed on.

Microphones, Sound Systems, Blackboards

I have already discussed podiums with built-in sound systems. If your hotel has a podium for you that has no built-in amplification, and you feel that it is necessary, you will need to make arrangements to order a **microphone and sound system.** Consider the type of microphone needed. If the boss/instructor will be moving about the room, she might need a hand or lavalier microphone. If, in addition to walking around, she will need to have her hands free to demonstrate or emphasize her point, you should order a lavalier type. A lavalier microphone hangs around the neck and leaves the hands free. If she will be standing in one place and not using a podium, consider a microphone on an adjustable stand. Amplification will be achieved by plugging into an existing house sound system (you will have to ask your hotel contact if there is a sound system in your particular meeting room), or by ordering a separate sound system. Check on the costs of these alternatives. It might behoove you to order a self-contained standing podium.

First of all, let me explain that **blackboards** have changed through the years. Now they might be black, green, or white. The black and green boards still use chalk and erasers. Be sure the hotel includes your chalk and erasers on the contract. (Otherwise the set-up personnel might forget them.)

White boards have become very popular. Your boss/instructor will use a special marker on this type of board. It is a dry wipe-off type which the hotel will provide. *She must not use a permanent marker like she uses on the flip charts or she may end up buying the hotel a new white board!* A clean dry cloth will be needed to make erasures on this type of board. Again, it will be the responsibility of the hotel to provide the proper cloth or eraser but it wouldn't be a bad idea to tuck a clean dry cloth into the boss' briefcase. Tell her it's in there just in case the hotel forgets to give her one.

You might want to inquire about available copying facilities. Ask if your boss will have access to a copier and if the charges can be applied to the master account. This is particularly important if you hold weekend meetings when administrative offices (and equipment) might be locked.

Chapter 8
Room in the Inn

Many of the meetings you book will have sleeping room requirements. Whether you need one room or one hundred rooms, the rules for making those reservations are basically the same.

Room Block

If you are booking a meeting, you are probably already in touch with someone in the sales department. They should be able to block the necessary rooms for you. If not, you will be referred back to someone in reservations. Even so, the procedure will be the same.

The number of sleeping rooms that you think you will need are to be blocked at the same time you book your meeting. Sleeping rooms may be blocked on a tentative or definite basis as are the meeting rooms.

If you are going to have fifty attendees at the meeting, and thirty-five are from out of town, you will want to block forty rooms. This will allow for any extra rooms that you might need. Perhaps your National Sales Manager decides (at the last minute of course) to attend your boss' meeting. You wouldn't want the hotel to be full and unable to accommodate him. Think ahead.

The hotel will almost always give you a cut off. (This is not a pair of ragged blue jeans . . .) A cut off is a date that is generally ten days to two weeks before the arrival date. It is a deadline to have the names to go with the number of rooms blocked. If you fail to deliver the names by the cut off, your entire block or the remaining block that does not have names with it will be dropped. This means that all rooms, or the rooms without names, are put back into the system to be sold to someone else. Do not take cut offs lightly. *communicate* *Always specify an even earlier cut off in your letter to your attendees.*

If your hotel will work with you, you may be able to reserve a few rooms past the cut off. They can be blocked in the company name for an additional few days in case the Big Boss needs a room (these guys are the hardest to plan for), or if some of the attendees change their minds and want to come at the last minute.

Types of Rooms

Most hotels have various types of accommodations. In addition to reserving the appropriate number of accommodations, you will need to be knowledgeable of the different types.

Single: This refers to one person in one bed. The type of bed may vary from a twin bed (I hope not) to a luxurious king size.

Double: This refers to two people in one bed. Most often this will apply to a married couple. They may occupy a double, queen, or a king size bed. Be careful not to block doubles for your attendees unless they plan to sleep together in the same bed!

Twin: This refers to two people in two beds. They may each occupy a twin, double, or maybe a queen size bed. This will be the category you will use when doubling-up your attendees.

Suites: Suites may be anything from a regular room with a separate sitting area to a plush multi-room penthouse! The type of beds may be anything from double to king size and the sky's the limit when it comes to amenities. If the Big Boss is impressed with this type of accommodation, by all means try to put him into one. Suites are always more expensive, (except in an "all suite" hotel) If your budget doesn't quite allow for an upgraded more expensive room, you might try doing a little negotiating to bring the rate down.

Location and Amenities

In addition to the types of rooms in each category, location and amenities may play an important role in determining the rooms you want to block.

Location may include inside, outside, upstairs, downstairs, poolside, main building, or tower. Ask questions and understand the different locations your particular hotel has to offer.

Amenities are special complimentary items or services sometimes offered with certain rooms. In the bathroom you might find designer shampoos, deodorants, shower caps, hair dryers and luxurious bathrobes. In the room itself, you could expect remote control television, an automated cocktail valet, an upgraded ice container (not your standard plastic bucket) or *turn-down service.*

Turn-down service means that a housekeeper will come to the room in the early evening and turn down the sheets of the bed, often leaving on the pillow a mint or a liqueur and a card wishing the guest "sweet dreams."

In connection with, but not necessarily in, the upgraded room, the hotel may offer a local newspaper at the door in the morning, or perhaps a continental breakfast served in a designated area reserved only for the guests of these rooms. Complimentary or discounted food and beverage may also be a part of this package.

A rapid check-in procedure may be an amenity that will save time, if not money. Some hotels offer check-in from a remote location. It may be a hotel desk at the airport or a car rental location. You can check in, go on to your business appointment, return to the hotel at any hour, needing only to stop at the desk to pick up a key.

communicate   Understand carefully the amenities included with the rooms you block. Be careful not to pay a substantial amount more for a room with amenities that will not be used or appreciated. For example, if you are planning a group breakfast for your participants, you won't need to reserve rooms that are more expensive because they include a continental breakfast. Communicate and use your common sense. Remember: all of these frills and extras are a way for the hotel to increase room revenue at a modest cost to themselves. Use moderation when reserving these higher cost rooms.

Room Rates and Negotiating Them

Room rates vary enormously! The only advice I can offer you is to shop the hotels in the area you prefer. As I said, rates should be fairly competitive within an area.

You should not pick a hotel based solely on rates,

but rates must surely be a factor. If you need rate consideration, that is, if you feel your budget won't allow the quoted rate, you must tell your hotel contact. (The worst thing that can happen is that they'll say "no".) Hotels grant sleeping room rate consideration based on the same things as meeting room charge consideration. They will look at the revenue generated by this meeting. They will consider future business you might take elsewhere if they do not meet your demands this time. *communicate*

Hotels will be more easily swayed if it is their off season. This may apply to months of the year or days of the week. Don't forget, a business hotel that is full during the week may be more than willing to negotiate rates for a weekend meeting. You may find a substantial reduction for state and federal government meetings. Consider whether your group fits into these categories.

Arrival and Departure Dates

When you request a block of rooms, you will have to specify an arrival and a departure date. Unless you know differently at this point, you will block everyone with the same arrival and departure date. (Later on, you might find that you will have some coming in early or some staying longer.) If you know they are individual arrivals, say so. If by any chance your group is arriving by bus, please inform the hotel so they may staff accordingly.

Room Guarantees

Hotels have various rules regarding holding rooms for late arrival. It has been my experience that 6:00 P.M. seems to be the magic hour. Rooms held after this hour will need to be guaranteed.

You can guarantee a room for late arrival by the use of a major credit card or to your company account. Please be forewarned that guaranteeing rooms means just that. Should you have any persons not show up and you have guaranteed their rooms, be prepared to pay for those rooms.

Cancellations need to be made before 6 P.M. and be sure to get a cancellation number or the name of the hotel employee with whom you cancel the res-

communicate   ervation. Again, I would advise you to discuss hotel policy on this.

Who Pays for What?

Now that we know how many rooms, what type of rooms, and about guaranteeing those rooms for late arrival, we must consider who will pay for what.

Sometimes your company will pay for all rooms, tax, and incidentals. (Incidentals are individual meals, phone calls, room service, bar charges, laundry or gift shop items.) Don't tell the hotel you will be responsible for everything unless you are prepared to cover all the items listed above. (You could end up paying for the "adorable pink teddy bear" Mr. Smith buys as a trip present for his little girl.)

You may want to limit what your company will be responsible for. Perhaps your company will pay for room and tax only. Individuals will be responsible for their own incidental charges. In this case, upon cheek-in, your attendees will be asked for a major credit card to cover any incidentals charged to their sleeping room. If they cannot produce a major credit card or do not put up a cash deposit to cover estimated incidental charges, they must pay as they go and cannot charge anything to their room. All hotels have a system to notify their "outlets" (lounge, restaurants, gift shops) of the names of the guests who are not permitted to charge anything to their room.

You may want to pay for incidentals except bar charges. In this case I would recommend that you advise your attendees not to charge any liquor to their sleeping rooms. If, after that, they still charge liquor to their room, you should pay it with the master account bill and after the meeting, get reimbursed by the employee. Your boss can then speak with the employee about the matter and it will prevent any confrontations at the hotel front desk.

Another way of handling charges is to have the individuals pay for everything (rooms, tax, and incidentals, that is). All attendees in this case will be asked for a major credit card upon arrival. They can then charge all incidentals to their room and, when they check out, all expenses including room and tax each night will be paid by them. Your attendees will then probably turn in an expense report for the amount they are to be reimbursed by your company.

Chapter 9

Feeding the Masses

As you and your boss are discussing the meeting room seating arrangements, sleeping room accommodations and audio-visual needs, you will also want to talk about any group or "planned" meals you want to have.

How Many Meal Functions?

Let's say you are having a two day meeting. You might want to set up a group lunch each day. A dinner on one of the evenings would be nice with a cocktail reception prior to the dinner, held in a separate room, the same room, or by the pool! (Feel your imagination going to work?) I am not trying to make money for the hotel by suggesting these functions. You will be entirely on your own to decide how many functions you will sponsor.

Blocking Space, Seating Arrangements

Once you decide on the meals you want to set up, be sure to block rooms of ample size to eat those meals in. The most popular types of seating arrangements for meal functions are rounds or U-shape.

It has been my experience that a change of pace is nice here. If your group has met all day in a U-shape put them at rounds for their meals. If they have been at a conference table, put them at a U-shape. A class-room set-up for a meeting may lend itself to rounds or a U-shape for the meal functions.

Choosing Menus and Giving Guarantees

If you don't already have banquet menus (you'll usually get those on your site inspection, which will be covered in depth in Chapter 13), request them at the time you reserve your space. Make a follow-up note to yourself as to when you should have them. You should look them over carefully and be sure you know what you are ordering. Don't be intimidated by entrees with fancy names. Ask questions. You may find that your hotel contact may not know exactly what a certain item is. They will find out for you if you inquire. Then you can choose your menus intel-ligently.

follow-up

You will be required to give the hotel a guarantee on all meals forty-eight hours prior to the particular function. A guarantee is a final count of the number of attendees and a guarantee that you will pay for that many meals.

The hotel will prepare for a certain amount over your guarantee. (Check with your hotel contact on this number. It is usually ten percent.) That means if you guarantee fifty persons, they will prepare enough food for fifty-five persons. Be advised however, that if you have only forty-five persons show up, you will be charged for your guaranteed number. If your contact says they have a ten percent leeway, it usually means upward only. You cannot lower your guarantee once you are within the forty-eight hour period. (Some hotels even require as long as seventy-two hours on guarantees.) Know also that buffet meals often require minimum guarantees of fifty persons.

When choosing menus, keep in mind any special dietary needs. Your attendees should be told in the notification letter that they must inform you of any special needs. You can give them examples, like food allergies, low-sodium diets, vegetarian needs, etc.

Choosing menus should not be a chore. Choose carefully and it will pay off. Keep your lunch selections on the lighter side and save the intense rich food for the evening meals. Some hotels offer a working lunch. This is great for a small, intense meeting that is short on time and long on items to be covered.

This menu is light, usually an assortment of sandwiches, chips, desserts or fruit, and a beverage. It is served on a rolling cart that is brought into the meeting room approximately ten minutes before the scheduled lunch break. The attendees help themselves at the specified time, return to their meeting table, and the meeting goes on while they eat. Again, not all hotels offer working lunches and they are appropriate only for small groups.

Be considerate when deciding on menus. Do not have beef at every meal. Alternate with chicken and fish. Generally, you will be asked to choose appetizers, entrees, and desserts from a standard list. Usually, bread and butter, coffee or tea, and vegetables and/or potatoes are also included in the price of the banquet meal.

Be careful with vegetables offered as "chefs choice" or "vegetable of the day." (A phrase like this places you literally at the mercy of the hotel.) It usually isn't too bad but remember—you might be opening yourself up for THE INFAMOUS BANQUET GREEN PEA! (Green peas have been served at banquets since the dawn of time; usually overcooked or undercooked, seldom tasting just right.) Ask what types of vegetables the chef usually prepares with the particular entree you have chosen. If you don't want a certain vegetable, tell your contact. Impress on them, for instance, that you do not want broccoli or green peas as the green vegetable. On the contract it may look like this:

French onion soup
Fresh garden salad, choice of dressing
Sliced london broil
Vegetable of the day (No broccoli or green peas)
Parsleyed new potatoes
Rolls and butter
Key lime pie
Coffee, Tea

If your special requests are not clearly spelled out on the contract, feel free to write in any clarification before signing and sending it back.

When choosing menus, try to choose the dishes that will please the most people. Banquet meals are sometimes difficult to choose when you have no idea what your people like. Do the best you can. Be sure, however, to consider your boss' preference or his boss' preference. If the Big Boss is coming in for the day, or maybe just lunch, you wouldn't want to order fresh snapper if he is allergic to fish. His secretary may be able to help you in this area. Be sure to get a final OK on the menu from your own boss.

Creative Breaks

You will also need to make arrangements for breaks. A break should be planned as carefully as a full meal. They are not difficult to set up and add so much to the mood of the meeting.

Your meeting should (at the very least) begin with coffee. If you are going to save money and cut corners, please don't scrimp on the coffee. I have seen grown men cry upon entering a conference room and finding it void of coffee. They may have just come from a large breakfast and had three cups of the stuff, but there is something sacred about having coffee available in the meeting room. What about the poor soul who is running late? He slides into the room just as the door is being closed and can't make it through the morning without that life-giving cup of coffee.

Coffee is sold by the gallon. Sound like an enormous amount? Guess again . . . one gallon of coffee serves approximately eighteen to twenty cups. For a group of ten that's two cups to last two to three hours.

Ask yourself if the quantity fits your particular group. You may know that four of your attendees do not drink coffee. Fine. Be sure to order some juice, but remember that the coffee drinkers will also help themselves to the juice. (Don't get discouraged . . . Your hotel contact will be able to help you in these areas.) Being knowledgeable of quantities and their yields will protect you from the overzealous hotel employee who tries to sell you four gallons of coffee when two will suffice.

The addition of doughnuts, danish, muffins or biscuits will further please the hungry types in the group. (I know, I'm one of them . . .)

Afternoon breaks can be fun. I suggest individual fresh fruit cups, granola bars, cookies, sherbet, and some groups enjoy creating their own ice cream sundaes. Don't forget to add some soft drinks in the afternoon (regular and diet) as well as a small quantity of coffee.

I guess what I'm trying to get across here is that you can let loose your imagination when it comes to breaks. There have been too many dull and boring meetings interspersed with the same kind of breaks. It will be up to your boss to add "zing" to the meeting, but you can give life to the breaks. Make sure there is variety in the breaks you set up. Tell the hotel what you would like to do. They might need to get back to you with a price. That's okay. Be persistent. Don't take "no" for an answer. Generally a hotel will be able to accommodate any reasonable request for a specified cost.

communicate

follow-up

In addition to the menus and the seating, you also need to talk to the boss about budgets. (No, I don't mean your salary projections for the next three years). If you have a dollar amount to spend on meals, discuss it.

Meal Prices

If it looks like your budget will allow only peanut butter sandwiches for lunch you might reconsider having group lunches at the hotel.

When you receive the hotel menus and prices, don't faint dead away. Remember: These prices are always higher than a la carte prices in a restaurant. You are paying for a private dining room and a private serving staff. Prices may not include tax and tip. Read the fine print.

Banquet tips or gratuities are generally one or two percent higher than the standard restaurant gratuity. You will probably have to add your state tax and the banquet gratuity to the cost of each meal. This multiplied by the number of attendees will give you the cost of one meal function. If you find that some meals don't fall within your budget guidelines, discuss this with your contact. They may be able to come up with a menu that is workable for both of you.

You Cannot Bring It In

One last point to remember: Most hotels will not permit any food or beverages to be brought into public areas. They are in business to make money and these are two areas in which they do just that.

Now that we have taken a good look at food arrangements, let's discuss liquor and when and how to purchase it.

Chapter 10

What about Liquor?

Meetings and liquor sometimes do not mix. Your boss will have definite ideas on this. Get specific instructions from him regarding any liquor arrangements you are to make. Since liquor can be a very expensive area of your meeting I want to make every effort to cover as many variations as possible.

Hotels sell liquor "by the bottle" or "by the drink". "Bottle" sales lend themselves well to large groups. A "by the drink" situation can work well in large or small groups. Let me show why one works better than the other in some cases.

Bottle Sales — Pros and Cons

Bottle liquor can at first seem terribly expensive. Fifty dollars plus tax and tip is not an unreasonable amount for a liter size bottle of a name brand liquor! Fifty dollars!!! Why . . . fifty dollars must be four or five times what you can buy this bottle for at the nearby neighborhood liquor store. Granted, it probably is. But, you must remember that you cannot bring that ten to twenty dollar bottle into the hotel to serve at your cocktail party. Liquor sales are a high profit area for the hotel, one that helps to offset other non-profit areas. Bottle prices seem high, but let's look at what you are getting for your money.

Remember, you can only compare bottle prices to your other alternative, which is by the drink.

Consider this: A liter size (33.8 oz) bottle will serve approximately thirty (1 oz) drinks. (If a machine measured them out it would serve 33.8 drinks . . . but I'm betting your attendees would rather have a real live person serving them.) If you bought those same thirty drinks on a per drink basis at $2.50 per drink you would pay $75.00 plus tax and tip. The bottle purchase was more economical. Bottle sales are conducive to large groups. Let's look at why.

In the above example we poured drinks from only one bottle; one kind of liquor. In reality, if you purchase by the bottle, you will probably start with at least a bottle each of bourbon, scotch, gin, vodka, a blend, and perhaps a rum. You will be charged for every one of these that are open at the end of the hour (or whatever the specified time is for the cocktail party). Even if they have only one drink poured from them, you will be charged for them. Some hotels contract for a certain amount of bottles, whether opened or not, but I think most will take back any unopened bottles.

What happens to the partially full bottles? They are the responsibility of the purchasing party. Take them. Have your boss take them home or give them to someone in your group. At any rate, take them—

you have paid for them. How much have you paid for them? Somewhere in the neighborhood of three hundred dollars (if you didn't order any more of any type of liquor and at least one drink was poured from each of the six bottles and you chose the name brand liquor). How many drinks did you serve?

You can figure an average of two drinks per person per hour.

This is only an estimate as some will drink more but some will drink less. You had 75 persons at the party. If they had been drinking on a per drink basis they would have consumed approximately 150 drinks at $2.50 each, or $375. Sounds like bottle sales was the best route. But, be careful; there are hidden risks in bottle sales. You could conceivably end your cocktail hour with six (or even more) bottles which had only a drink or two poured from them. You will have purchased the entire bottle for $50 to $75, making those one or two drinks very expensive. Someone will take those bottles home, of course, but it greatly increases the per capita costs for the cocktail party and money is needlessly spent.

If you do choose the bottle route, you might try offering only three kinds of liquor, as well as beer and wine. Be very strict about the replenishment of that liquor. Communicate to the banquet coordinator *communicate* exactly who may sign for additional bottles. Tell them you are not paying for any unauthorized replenishment. Any additional bottles may be added only by this person. (Have this spelled out in the contract.) *follow-up* Unless you have been at this for a while, opt for the open bar on a per drink basis.

I have seen bartenders and banquet personnel badgered by guests purporting to be the "president" of the company. They would order additional bottles of liquor and threaten to take all their future business elsewhere if their demands were not met! A simple "yea" or "nay" from the designated contact will eliminate any possibility of trouble and free the bartender of any embarrassment.

Suppose that "guy" who says "I think we need another bottle of Bourbon" really is the president of the company. The bartender may simply catch the eye of the designated contact and get authorization. They will also have him sign for additional bottles. Even the president should appreciate a tightly controlled, well-run cocktail party. The designated contact will also want to control the ordering of additional bottles too close to the end of the cocktail party, thus reducing the likelihood of leftover bottles.

Open Bars, Cash Bars, Bartenders

Another way to cut down on misunderstandings or the possibility of disputes over a liquor bill would be to have an **open bar** on a per drink, rather than whole bottle basis. This will be for a specified length of time and your company will be responsible for paying for drinks served during this time.

The bar will offer a variety of liquor, including beer (regular and light) and wine (rose and chablis). This type of set up will require a bartender supplied by the hotel. There may be a bartender charge depending on the amount of liquor sales your bar generates.

communicate   Get these charges, if any, understood and in writing from the hotel.

In the meeting planners kit you may have received from the hotel you will see that open bar prices are plus tax and tip ("plus-plus" as we call it in the industry). These items will be added on to your total liquor bill. Your bill will be based on the amount of liquor poured. In other words, the food and beverage director will issue liquor to the bartender at the beginning of the function. A careful record will be made of the amount that goes to the bar as well as any additions after the party begins. Afterwards, the bar is carefully checked for the amount of liquor that remains. Your contact may certainly be involved in the issuing of the liquor and the final count at the end of the party. Communication and follow-up must work side by side. The difference will be the amount of liquor your guests consumed. Your bill will be prepared from these findings.

There is another type of bar. This is called a **cash bar.** A cash bar requires that each person pay for their drinks. They may purchase tickets from a cashier and then trade the tickets for a drink at the bar or they may pay the bartender directly. Drink prices are rounded to include tax and tip. Thus, a cash bar drink price might be on the contract as "$2.75 inclusive". Beer and wine may be "$2.00 inclusive". Cash bars are generally set up by associations and only occasionally by corporations. A variety of liquor should still be offered as well as beer and wine. A bartender charge will apply on a cash bar so be sure to understand how much it will be.

If your company does not comfortably fit into either of these categories you might consider a combination of each. Your company might agree to pay for no more than two drinks per person. Each attendee can be given two tickets for drinks. Once these two drink tickets are used, your attendees will be required to pay cash for any additional drinks. Your company will be charged for the number of drinks equaling the number of tickets purchased.

Hors d'Oeuvres

At this point I would like to make a recommendation. If you offer liquor, offer food. Always have something to nibble even if it is just peanuts and potato chips (this would be perfectly acceptable if your attendees are going to be seated for dinner right after the cocktail hour). Fresh fruit and cheese trays can be a welcome and attractive addition to any cocktail party!

For a cocktail reception that will not be followed by a planned dinner, or one that will extend past one hour, you should order more heavily on the hors d'oeuvres. For cold hors d'oeuvres you might order fruit and cheese trays, fresh vegetables with dip, and perhaps some other fancy canapes. Your hot hors d'oeuvres selection might include Chinese egg rolls (always a favorite), rumaki (chicken liver and water chestnuts wrapped in bacon), and the old stand-by "chicken drummettes" or "wings of heaven."

When ordering hors d'oeuvres be sure to understand how many pieces you are getting. Most are sold by the tray which may contain 25 pieces or 50 pieces or just be spelled out as serving "X" amount of people. A good rule to follow is that you will need 6 pieces per person per hour. Of course, there may be some exceptions, so plan accordingly. If your cocktail reception is not followed by a dinner and will run through most peoples' dinner time, expect them to make a meal of the hors d'oeuvres and boost your estimate to say, 10 pieces per person per hour. For example, if you have 50 attendees at a one hour cocktail reception not followed by dinner, you will need to order enough trays of hors d'oeuvres to equal a total of three to five hundred pieces.

You owe it to your attendees to provide ample food at a cocktail party. You will reduce the chances of disorderly behavior and, more importantly, decrease the chances of alcohol-related driving accidents.

That just about covers the areas of food and beverage. I hope that I have impressed on you how important it is to *communicate* your specific needs to the hotel contact particularly in these areas. Your contact will welcome the knowledge that you are new at this and may need his or her advice and suggestions along the way.

Chapter 11

Send Me The Bill

"Send me the bill," the boss yells back over her-shoulder as she is leaving the hotel.

"But that's just not possible!" answers the conference manager with a look of consternation on her face. "Your contract clearly states that all charges will be paid on departure. You have not made any arrangements for credit."

"My credit is good all over this country! What do you mean arrangements?" the boss snaps back as she inches closer to the door.

"Yes, I'm sure you have good credit. However, it is the policy of this hotel ..."

"Listen, I stay at these hotels all the time. I charge everything for the meeting including my room and they send me a bill!" Interrupts the boss, finally standing still.

"I understand," replies the frazzled hotel employee. "However, it is usually left up to the individual hotel to establish credit policies."

She is starting to get edgy about the possibility that this bill might not get paid and her job may be on the line. She tries to remember; "Did her secretary set it up this way? Did I discuss credit with her secretary? No one to blame but myself just now. Don't want to make her angry over this . . . might not come back."

"Okay, I'll pay it this time. But my card is already close to its limit. What do you need from me?" asks the boss already fishing for her wallet and credit card. "But believe me, I'm not going to do this every time. If you can't bill me, I'm not coming back."

"I will send a credit application to your office immediately. I do apologize for the inconvenience." says the conference manager feeling very relieved.

If you had been at the scene as an invisible observer, you probably would never have set up another meeting as long as you lived!

You had worked so hard to be sure every detail was taken cared of; every "t" crossed and every "i" dotted. You thought you had done a magnificent job and everything had been letter perfect. You had communicated and followed-up time and again, but you had not satisfied the billing requirements.

Let's look back at what should have taken place to prevent the scene I just described. Our journey begins at the heart of the matter, the accounting office.

Meet The Controller and His Helpers

The accounting office controls the life-blood of the hotel. Every department operates within the guidelines set forth by the Controller and his two helpers "Reason" and "Logic".

Hotel controllers expect perfection from all other hotel employees. They also expect perfection from those of us who book with them.

Now that you know what the hotel personnel, especially the sales department, are up against, let's move along to examine what some of these policies are.

Folios, Master Accounts, Charges

I'm sure you are familiar with the term **master account.** What you may not be aware of is that "master account" does not refer to a form of payment. (It is not an authorization to send you a bill after the meeting.) It is merely a folio, or piece of paper, in your company name upon which all group charges are posted during your meeting.

Group charges are meeting room costs, company-paid group meals or cocktail parties, charges for audiovisual equipment and any other charges authorized by you or your boss to go onto that account. (If the president of the company will be in attendance, there's a good chance you might want to pick up, *or pay for,* all *of his charges.)*

Additionally, each occupied sleeping room will have a **folio** assigned to it upon which room and tax will be posted. Incidental charges incurred by the individual will also appear on this folio. Okay, let's look at that again. There will be a master account folio in your company name. There will be a folio for each attendees' sleeping room and incidental charges. The attendees might be responsible for paying for some of these charges, or your company might be paying for everything (As we discussed on page 56).

On Departure vs. Direct Billing

When you book your meeting you will need to determine how your company wishes to pay for the charges. They may pay on departure or be direct billed.

If the choice is **on departure** be sure the boss is aware of this and approves. He will be required to settle the bill at the end of the meeting by using a major credit card or company check. Do ask ahead of time if a company check will be acceptable and if there are any special identification requirements.

Credit Applications

If the choice is **direct billing,** it will necessitate an account being set up in your company name. Most likely, all that will be required is a credit application. Basically, the Controller (or Reason, or Logic) will be most interested in information on a previous hotel that extended credit to you. They will contact this hotel and determine if your company paid its bill within the terms of the agreement (usually thirty days). If you provide all necessary information and your credit is good elsewhere, chances are that this hotel will approve your application.

This process needs to be handled in a very timely manner as you must have approval prior to the beginning of your meeting. If it looks like there might not be *communicate* enough time to handle all of this by mail, ask whether you can give credit information over the phone. The accounting office can then make their inquiries over the phone, and the process may take no more than a few hours. This might not be acceptable to the hotel for one reason or another, or your credit may not be approved. In this case, you will need to have your boss pay on departure as discussed above. If time is

the enemy, go ahead and have a credit application
sent to you so you can return it and, hopefully, have   *follow-up*
an account set up before your next meeting. Communication and follow-up are essential here.

Exceptions to the Rule

If you'll recall, the Controller's helpers were not
called "Consideration" and "Understanding". Generally the accounting office, with the approval of the
General Manager, will make the rules regarding credit
and expect everyone to abide by them.

The Controller will seldom make exceptions to the
rules. If he does, it is generally with the understanding that the hotel employee who asks for special
consideration for their particular client will be the
guest of honor at the next sacrificial rites ceremony
if the bill is not paid. Get my drift? Please get your
paperwork in on time. Give them what they want.

You might compare their requests to your company's policies on extending credit. Maybe their
requests are not so unreasonable after all.

Chapter 12

Special Types of Meetings

On occasion, you may be called upon to set up a special type of meeting. One that is a deviation from the usual business meeting you are used to.

These meetings could be computer meetings, trade or continuity shows, training seminars and/or continuing education programs, contractor bid teams, themed parties, or fashion shows, just to name a few.

These meetings will still have the basic requirements: meeting or display space, sleeping rooms, and meal functions. They should be handled in the same fashion as you normally would handle your Board of Directors meeting, with a few exceptions. These meetings will have special requirements to make them run smoothly.

I won't spend a lot of time in these areas, but let's look briefly at what makes each one so unique.

Computer Meetings

A computer meeting will generally be a training session. Each student may be set up at a table all to themselves allowing enough room for their CRT (monitor), keyboard, possibly a printer, and training materials. (Allow some room for elbows too.) All students will generally face forward to watch a large screen (with a video presentation) or the instructor.

Pay particular attention to the need for numerous electrical outlets throughout the meeting room. Each computer and each printer will need its own three-prong outlet. One more quick suggestion: Be sure to invest in some sort of "spike protection" when setting up computers in a hotel meeting room. You can purchase an electrical outlet "bar" that will serve as a buffer against unexpected surges of electricity, power failures, and electrical storms. It would not be a bad idea if you could make sure the hotel contact informed their maintenance department that a computer class was in session. This might further eliminate any unnecessary line interruptions.

Trade Shows

Trade shows require a lot of space and electrical outlets become a factor again. Individual areas, usually at least eight feet by eight feet, will be sectioned off, often in the hotel's main ballroom. Sectioning is accomplished by using stanchions and draping. Large hotels may have these available, others will have to contract with a company that specializes in the physical set-up of this type of show, that is, the actual setting up of portable walls, stanchions, draping and any additional electrical needs. The costs involved will be passed on to you with, I might add, a hefty surcharge for the hotel handling it. You might want to deal directly with that company. Your local yellow pages will be a good source for finding a company that will do the job for you.

Consider also local organizations who do nothing but set up trade shows in their entirety. These organizations will book the exhibit space, negotiate rooms and rates, and coordinate your show from start to finish. Look in your phone book under "Trade Shows" or "Expositions".

Continuity Shows

A continuity show might be set up by you if you work for a company that offers promotional items to its customers. A grocery chain is a good example of this. For instance, if your company's stores offer items such as dishes or books, or if they sell housewares or toys, your corporate buyers are probably bombarded regularly for appointments by various manufacturers of these items. To alleviate some of the crunch, you might want to set up a continuity show whereby selected vendors from all over the country might be invited by your company to participate. They will come to your specified location, and set up their displays that feature the newest, hottest items to be released in the upcoming months. They will be allowed on an individual basis to give your top buyers their best sales pitch!

You and your boss will have to decide how big the show will be. Will it encompass two days with fifty invited vendors or will it be one day with twenty-five vendors? You will be responsible for making all the arrangements with the hotel. I suggest that you send a letter to prospective attendees noting that space is limited. Ask them to reply within a specified time as to the number of representatives they will be sending (usually two to five); what their sleeping requirements are; and, most important, an estimate of how many pounds of merchandise they will be shipping prior to their arrival. This information will allow the hotel to staff accordingly.

I survived a few continuity shows. There are those conference managers, less fortunate than myself, who probably got out of the hotel industry altogether thanks to a continuity show!

I had the advantage of having a very knowledgeable corporate secretary who guided me through the first show of this kind. Together we put on a good show. It was not without its problems but, as we did it again and again over about a four year period, the shows became a real pleasure to be involved with and generated a considerable amount of money for my hotel.

Continuity shows require a lot of work for both the corporate secretary and the hotel personnel.

The main problem will be the fact that the vendors will need to ship merchandise to the hotel well ahead of their scheduled arrival. And I do mean a lot of merchandise! You and your boss will work with the hotel to establish the earliest allowable shipping date and the latest allowable pick up date for this merchandise. We found over the years that if you are firm with the vendors, they will abide by the rules you set forth.

Storage of merchandise for as much as three weeks prior to the show becomes a monumental problem. This could be discussed at length with your hotel contact. They may arrange for a meeting room to become the storage area, but expect some discussion on compensation. We finally came to an agreement on a vendor fee which could be passed on to the vendor to offset the amount of revenue lost by the hotel while using the room for storage.

Continuity shows mean "big bucks" for the lucky vendors whose merchandise is selected for regional or national distribution by the home office buyers. It is an excellent means to benefit both buyer and seller.

Training Seminars

If your company sponsors **training seminars** or continuing education programs for the general public, your approach will be somewhat different.

You will be blocking meeting space and sleeping rooms in various locations, often without benefit of knowing exactly how many you need. In order to more intelligently block space, you will need to consider several variables.

The type of seminar being presented will give you a clue as to the possible turnout. Will it appeal to only a specialized group of people or will the general public be interested in it? If a similar seminar has been presented at a similar location, you might also consider those attendance figures.

Are you offering this seminar in a large metropolitan area, where you will draw from nearby cities as well, or is it in a more remote, possibly even rural, location?

What will the weather be like at the time of the seminar? Northern locations can be difficult in the winter for both attendees and instructors.

Once you have determined the type of seminar and where you would like to present it, contact various hotels in those areas, much as you would contact local hotels. The key difference lies in the fact that the attendees will be responsible for making all their own hotel reservations. You might block a group of rooms with a two week cutoff and even negotiate a special rate, but your liability ends there. Do not guarantee these sleeping rooms.

You will design a flyer or brochure naming the location and the dates when the seminar or program will be offered. The brochure will also furnish all information needed on how to register, in writing or by phone; registration fees; and hotel reservation information. It will detail the format, location, and hours of the seminar. Your company will need to use extensive mailing lists to reach prospective attendees in a timely manner.

Contractor Bid Teams

Another special group are **general contractors** who send bid teams to various hotels across the country to bid on nearby construction projects. If you need to book this type of group, you will only have one major problem . . . telephone lines.

As before, all arrangements are handled the same as a regular meeting except for the telephones and lines.

You must find a hotel that can give your group an average of eight direct outside telephone lines installed, generally, in one meeting room.

Don't be surprised if the hotel contact is not too eager to book your group (we tend to be afraid of things we don't understand).

You will need to tell your hotel contact exactly how many lines you need. Be sure they comprehend the importance of the telephone lines. Impress on them that you need to know if the lines are available in the area. They will not normally have this information without calling the telephone company (unless they have booked contractor bid teams before).

communicate   Communicate until you feel confident that you can work with this hotel and be reasonably assured that you will get what you need. Then discuss a very special type of room arrangement.

The room arrangement will generally be tables against the walls with a chair and a telephone per attendee. Your bid team will spread blueprints and papers all over the place. Be sure to order ashtrays and large trash cans.

You will set up billing and connect/disconnect dates directly with the local telephone company. If you need to lease telephone equipment, check with the phone company or your hotel contact. You might find that your bid teams generally carry a portable phone system from place to place with them. This will eliminate leasing equipment in an unfamiliar town. Stay in touch with your hotel contact through the installation and connection of phone lines. Charges for installation of lines and phones need to be in writing whenever possible.

Your bid team will be on these phones for days calling subcontractors and getting prices. Without working phones, they might as well not show up. I was told once that they could sleep in the parking lot, but they had to have those telephones. Follow-up without fail.

If your lot in life is to book these bid teams, you *follow-up* have my sympathy. You live in a world of constant change. Your teams are always on the move and last minute changes are the rule and not the exception. Follow-up will definitely be the key to success with these groups. *follow-up*

Personally, I found these bookings to be a real challenge and after a lot of research and working with many patient and tolerant contractors and their secretaries, began to actively solicit their business. Finding a hotel contact who realizes the value of your business and is eager to work with you is indeed like finding buried treasure!

Themed Parties

Another corporate function you may need to know about is the themed party. This could be anything from an elaborate Las Vegas Night to a Country and

Western Bar-B-Que with cloggers and a hay ride.

When booking a themed party, consult your hotel contact as to what **packages** they have to offer. Packaged parties are going to be more economical than if you construct one of your own. Packaged theme parties will include such things as food, drink, decorations, costumed employees, props, sets, and backdrops. Generally, your per person charge will be less than if you try to supply all of these things from separate sources. If you do put a themed party together yourself, watch your expenses carefully. Themed parties can easily run into the thousands of dollars depending on how elaborate they are. Remember, atmosphere is very important. You must not underestimate the importance of decorations. Be sure the package they offer is packed with atmosphere and good food. Then, no matter what the theme, your party will be a success.

Tours and Fashion Shows

If the attendees will be bringing their spouses you might need to arrange for something for them to do one of the days during the meeting. This might be a tour of the city or nearby points of interest, a shopping extravaganza, or perhaps a poolside fashion show. This can best be accomplished by having the hotel give you some suggestions. They might suggest a local travel service who can help you plan a half day historical tour followed by an afternoon of shopping complete with transportation and shopping tips. You and your hotel contact can certainly plan a morning of tennis or a round of golf in combination with a poolside luncheon and fashion show. Don't forget to include the latest fashions for both men and women. A local department store should be willing to oblige.

Whether your luncheon and fashion show will

be held in the inside or outside (the weather does have a way of spoiling poolside functions), make sure that the tables are placed so that all participants have a clear view of the runway or stage. Do have an adequate sound system and proper lighting. The show coordinator or emcee will need a podium and microphone placed off to one side on the runway or stage. Spotlights can be placed every six feet or so at the edges of the. runway, angled toward the models, but not so high as to shine in their eyes.

Remember, these meetings are special. Most hotels are not booking them on a day-to-day basis. It is particularly important that you adhere to the rules of communication and follow-up.

Chapter 13

Choosing A Site

It would be my guess that at this point you are beginning to feel more relaxed about booking meetings, maybe even a little overconfident about your newly acquired wisdom. Don't . . . not until you read this chapter very carefully.

If you will recall, we discussed the three key players and their roles very early in the book. Let's think back to that chapter. We learned about each person's responsibilities to the success of the meeting.

You, as a key player, are obviously concerned about the success of the meetings you book or you would not even be reading this book.

I will agree, also, that there isn't much you can do as far as getting the boss to alter his course of action (at least not overnight). We would like to have his cooperation more often, his communication more timely, and his compliments less few and far between. This will come in time. For now, we will have to set aside any ambitions of radical change and concentrate on the things we have more control over.

The third key player we discussed was the hotel contact. Let me tell you right now that no matter how knowledgeable you become and however well-meaning your intentions, you will be defeated before you begin if you do not select a hotel that can and will follow your specific directions.

Criteria for Choosing

You do have some control over site selection. If we suppose that you currently have no favorite hotel (or that you are displeased with your current one), then there is a need to look objectively at the criteria for choosing a hotel. Some considerations are:

1. Location
2. Price
3. Quality of service
4. Quality of food
5. Your friend recommends it
6. Your relative works there
7. Club for Secretaries
8. Club for Bosses
9. Lively Lounge/Good Band
10. Tennis, Racquetball, Fitness room

In this day and age of creative advertising everyone claims that their product or services are the best. It is hard to know who will do the best job for you. Do not, however, base your selection solely on any of the above. You should, in fact, choose a site based on a combination of several of the amenities listed. A convenient location coupled with sensible prices, good food, and a friendly professional staff will be a winner!

It should be secondary that they have the hottest local band (most of your attendees might not even go into the lounge), or the best Secretary or Boss[7] Club. You should not be swayed by the mere fact that, based on your projected amount of meeting business, by this time next year you and your spouse could be winging your way to Acapuico, compliments of the hotel (I never said this would be easy) or that they try to lure you to them by offering tennis, racquetball, or a fitness room (things which sound good on the surface but, in reality, may never be used due to lack of time).

A recommendation by a friend or business associate can be a very good place to start your search but not necessarily the final answer to your quest for a meeting site. Even though your friend may have thoroughly researched available meeting sites, their recommendation may not be the best hotel for your meeting needs.

Keep in mind the type of meeting you are setting up and its objective. Is it a short, compressed meeting with an "all work and no play" attitude? Or is it an effort to combine business with relaxation in a resort atmosphere? Airport properties can be great for quick in-and-out meetings. This kind of meeting has its advantages; the attendees get home to family and friends sooner. The other alternative, the resort location, works especially well if spouses, at least, are included. After deciding this, the first consideration in choosing a site will be location. If the majority of your attendees will be from the surrounding local areas, you will want to consider a centrally located hotel, one that is fairly equidistant from the majority of your attendees. If a majority of your attendees will be coming from out-of-town you might want to consider using an airport location. Whether they are driving or flying into the city, they can utilize an airport property.

Tips on Where to Start

Look in the phone book and make a list of hotels that meet your location requirements. List also any hotels you have heard about that seem to do a good job, even though they may not be the most convenient location. These hotels could have so much going for them that it would be worth the extra drive to hold your meeting there.

Perhaps you have had hotel sales representatives call on you or your boss from time to time. Dig out any information you might have on these hotels. They have at least expressed an interest in your overnight and meeting business through these sales representatives. Include in your list any hotels where you may have been an attendee at a successful function. It might have been a luncheon for your astronomy group or a seminar where you learned computer programming. Give them a call and ask for names of companies who are presently using their hotels and if you may call them for a reference. If the references check out to your satisfaction, then by all means consider these hotels when making your list.

The next factor that you must consider will be price. I want you to be an aware shopper. Shop for the best value, not necessarily the lowest price. Your best value will be a hotel that gives you the combination I spoke of earlier: a convenient location, sensible prices, good food, and a friendly professional staff. Sensible prices are those that fit into your corporate budget. They are prices that are comparable within a certain hotel chain. For example, if you have three Restful Inns in your town, their prices should be in line with each other, but not necessarily in line with the two larger hotels in the Benton Hotel chain.

Once you have narrowed the list of available hotels by considering location and price range you should choose three or so and call them.

Initial Contact

Getting in touch with the right person can be very important. Tell the hotel switchboard that you are interested in booking a meeting and you would like to speak to someone in the sales department. They may not have a sales department, but you will have stated your business clearly enough for the switchboard operator to decide who to connect you with. When someone answers, state your business again. They will tell you if you have the right department. (No sense going into detail if you have accidently been connected to the housekeeping department!)

Site Inspections

Once you have established that you are talking with someone who books corporate meetings, tell them you are contemplating having a meeting and would like to schedule a site inspection. Tell them up front that you are shopping hotels in the area and will be making recommendations based on your findings. They will set aside a time for you to come to the hotel and they will give you a tour. It is not uncommon for the hotel contact to invite you to be his/her guest for lunch. Please accept this invitation as it will afford you the opportunity to taste their food as well as taking the tour.

Plan these inspections on days that you can be away from the office. Extend a lunch hour or leave the office early one afternoon. Be on time for your appointment. Expect the hotel contact to do the same. Respect for each other's time is important to both of you and will get you started on the right foot.

During your tour you will want to keep your eyes and ears open. Look around you, listen to what people are saying, determine whether the atmosphere is friendly and whether the hotel is properly staffed. If you go into the sales office, note mentally whether there is an air of calm efficiency or mass confusion and chaos. This might be a clue as to how your meeting will be handled.

Pay particular attention to the meeting rooms. Give your contact an idea of how many people you will have at your meeting and ask to see an example of a room *communicate* your group would have. Don't forget to tell them the type of seating arrangement you will need.

Be sure to notice whether there is ample lighting and whether the windows in the meeting room (if any) can be opened for even more light. Note whether the room can be darkened for film presentations.

Discuss the adequacy of the heat and/or air conditioning. Inquire whether the meeting room has an individual thermostat to control the heat/air. If not, ask how the temperature is controlled. You can tell your boss whether he will either be able to adjust the meeting room temperature by himself or have to summon help from a hotel employee.

Notice also the cleanliness of the room. Do the carpets look and smell clean? Are the walls attractive with no obvious holes or scuff marks? Is the wallpaper attractive and intact? Are the banquet chairs clean and in good repair? Does their equipment, in general, appear to be in good condition?

Look at the ceiling tiles. If you see numerous water stains, they have or have had a leaking roof. A^k about the status of the leaks. If you are not satisfied that the leak has been fixed in that room, make it clear that you would rather see another room. Also make it clear that should you book your meeting here, you do not want your group in that room. If all the rooms have questionable ceilings, think twice about meeting there at all. You don't want your boss' meeting called on account of rain . . . inside the room!

A tour of the sleeping rooms can be very enlighten-
ing. A newly remodeled lobby does not necessarily
mean that the sleeping rooms are newly remodeled.
Don't make the mistake of being overwhelmed by a
spectacular front desk and lobby area only to overlook substandard sleeping rooms. Ask to be shown
the type of rooms your attendees will have. Get a
clear understanding of any amenities that go with
the rooms. Understand the rates and make a note of
them. Look at these rooms with the same scrutiny as
you did the rest of the hotel. Comfort and cleanliness
should be foremost on your list with a price you can
afford.

If you are invited to lunch you will want to observe
whether the food is prepared in a timely manner as
well as a tasty one. Do not get so involved in your
conversation that you overlook the fact that it took the
server twenty minutes to notice you, or that it took
forty-five minutes to prepare a tuna fish sandwich! If
you find that the service in the restaurant is slow, ask
about it. You will probably be told that they are short
of help that day, or that the banquet help is quicker
or whatever excuse seems to pop out at the moment.
At any rate, just asking will strengthen your "I-don't-
want-to-be-taken-advantage-of" attitude.

This will be a good time to note the cooking style of
the hotel chef. Generally, the same or similar cooking
style is reflected in the restaurants as in the banquet
meals. Although the specific menu items will differ,
you should be able to discern whether seasonings are
appropriate, portions are adequate, and presentation
is appealing. Additionally, your attendees will probably be eating some meals in this very restaurant aside
from those group meals you arrange. Having lunch
with your contact will afford you great insight if you
know what to look for.

I suggest that you ask as many questions and take

as many notes as time allows. You will want to refer back to those notes when you make your recommendations to the boss.

Establishing A Rapport

Last, but certainly not least, note the rapport you were able to establish with the hotel contact. Did you feel at ease talking to him/her? Was it easy for you to ask questions? Was there a sincere interest in making you feel at home and in the success of your upcoming meeting? If you can answer "yes" to most of these questions you will probably work well together. Be sure to mention to the boss whether you felt a strong rapport or not with certain hotels when you review your findings. You, after all, will be working very closely with this person and that rapport will be a very important, though intangible, element.

communicate

follow-up

After you have completed all site inspections, compile your notes in a neat and concise manner using a **site inspection report.** You'll find an example of one in the Appendix. Present these reports to the boss with notations of things you liked or disliked about each one. Spend some time together discussing these reports. If there are some things that are not clearly defined, get on the phone and get them straightened out.

Once you have decided where you want to hold your meeting and gathered all the necessary information, it will be time for you to put aside any doubts and fears, adopt a "chin up" attitude and plunge post-haste into the exciting world of meeting planning.

Let's go on an imaginary journey and look at some actual dialogue for an actual meeting . . . The one y offset up.

Chapter 14

Let's Put it on Paper

Telephone Dialogue — An Actual Booking

"Good Afternoon. Benton Hotels. May I help you?" The switchboard operator's voice sounded brisk and pleasant.

"I'd like to speak to Wendy Davis in the Sales Department."

"One moment please, I'll connect you."

While you waited to talk to Wendy, you quickly thought back to your recent tour of the Benton III hotel. It had not been the biggest or the most expensive one you had looked at. It really was quite middle-of-the-road. You looked at a hotel that was much newer and one that was a lot bigger. This had been your choice.

The decor of the Benton III was modern and very

tastefully done in shades of mauve and mist green. Accent pieces of brass and glass sparkled when they caught the reflection of light coming through the windows. The meeting rooms were clean and bright and offered all the basics. Their sleeping rooms had been priced only slightly higher than a comparable hotel down the road but had a much more inviting appearance. In general, the hotel had a warm hospitable atmosphere.

Then there was Wendy. She had seemed eager to please from the very first contact and on the day of your tour she had taken you under her wing. A self-assured, competent business woman, she had a helpful friendliness about her that you liked.

"Good afternoon, sales office, Wendy speaking."

"Hi Wendy . . . this is Marty Hawthorne."

"Oh, Ms. Hawthorne. How are you?" she interrupted, obviously remembering you from last week's tour. "Have you made your decision yet?" She asked hopefully.

"Yes, we want to have our meeting at the Benton III ..." You knew that would make her happy and hoped that the two of you could start making the arrangements right away.

"Oh good, lets get you in the book then. What were your dates?" Wendy was obviously very pleased we had chosen the Benton III.

That was also your cue . . . the magic words that indicated she was ready to book this thing with you and that it was time to see if you had done your homework.

How Many and When?

"It's a three day meeting—August 7th, 8th, and 9th. I'll need a meeting room for fifty people, set classroom style each day and a room for group lunches all three days. I want a poolside cocktail party and dinner the evening of the 7th. So-o-o I guess we'll also need a back-up room reserved in case of rain?" you said with an air of confidence.

"Yes, we will. Hey, didn't you tell me you hadn't set up a meeting before? Sounds like you know exactly what you need. That's great . . . hold on, let me check those dates for you."

While Wendy went to the function book to check the space, a tiny, yet proud, smile appeared unconsciously on your face. While waiting for her to return, you picked up your papers and carefully straightened them. You tried not to think about the fact that those dates might not be available.

After what seemed like an eternity, Wendy returned to the telephone.

"Okay ... we're all set. I have the space blocked for you. Do you have some times and other details for me?" Wendy inquired.

"I'll give you everything I have now on the meeting. Is it okay if I have some changes as we go along?" You really were quite sincere but your question brought laughter from the other end of the telephone.

"Is it okay? I'd be very surprised if you didn't have a lot of changes. Don't worry about that. I'm used to it." Wendy's tone changed from mild laughter to one of reassurance. "Listen, sometimes the final booking looks nothing like the original one! It should, but I realize that it is sometimes difficult to get all the information up front. I'm going to fill out a work order contract that will be typed and sent to you for your boss' signature. Let me ask you questions and you give me the answers. *communicate* If you don't know the answer, just make a note and check with the boss." Wendy suggested. *follow-up*

"This was going to be easy ..." you thought. You really didn't have time to be calling back and forth a dozen times.

The Basic Information

"Okay," Wendy continued, "I have the dates and estimated number of attendees. I'll go through each day of the meeting in case you have anything different from one day to the next. Lets start with the basic information. Your full company name and address?"

"Toys International, 3388 Unicorn Lane."

"Oh, that's appropriate," Wendy laughed. "And your zip code?"

"32210," you answered.

"We have a reader board in the lobby that will be posted each day of your meeting to direct your attendees to the proper rooms for meetings and meals. Do you want it to read 'Toys International'?"

"Yes, that will be fine."

"Telephone number? Oh, I have it here . . . 782-0018?"

"Yes, that's it." You remembered you had given it to her when you came out for the tour.

"Will you be my contact?" Wendy was writing as she asked these questions.

"For now, I will be. My boss' name is Mr. Moreland. He will be in charge of the meeting."

"Mr. Moreland?" Wendy repeated it back to you. "Spell that for me, would ya?"

"M-0-R-E-L-A-N-D" You spelled it slowly to her as you had done so many times for so many people. . . . It really was just as it sounded but so many people had trouble with it.

Meeting Space and Equipment Needs

"I have reserved the Washington Room all three days for your meeting ..."

"Is that the room I looked at?" You knew you had

interrupted her but you didn't want to forget to ask.

"Yes it is. Uh, and the Jefferson Room, which is comparable in size to the one you saw, each of the three days for lunch. What are the times you will need these rooms each day?"

"The meeting will run from nine until five each day. Lunches are from noon until one. What room do you have set aside for dinner on Wednesday, the 7th?" you inquired. You too were writing as you went.

"I thought the Jefferson Room would suffice as a back-up room. Hopefully we'll be poolside but you never know about this weather." Wendy's mind drifted momentarily to the one luau that was forced inside because of rain. It went off well enough but it just wasn't the same . . . something very special about eating outside. "All right, I have the Washington Room each day from nine to five; the Jefferson Room each day for lunch from twelve to one; and the Jefferson Room on Wednesday evening from ..." Her voice trailed off indicating she needed an answer.

"Oh, cocktails from six until seven o'clock and dinner from seven until . . . What do you think . . . nine o'clock?" you wondered.

"That's good. Okay I have that. Now, how about any audio-visual equipment? Will you need any projectors or flip charts?"

"Yes, I need to get a price from you on an overhead all three days and a slide projector on Thursday and Friday only."

"The projectors are $35.00 each, each day." The clicking noise at the other end signaled she was using her calculator for the totals. "So that's $175.00 plus 5 percent tax which is $183.75."

"One hundred eighty three dollars and seventy five cents." You repeated back to her. "Put us down for those and I'll let you know if the boss has a problem with that."

"Overhead Wednesday, Thursday, and Friday, and a slide projector on Thursday and Friday only." Wendy was carefully repeating everything back to you. You liked that.

"That just about does it for the meeting room needs. Oh, we furnish note pads and pencils and we'll put water pitchers, glasses, ashtrays and matches on the tables. If you think >of anything else you need for the meeting room, you can just call me. May I make some arrangements for your breaks?" Wendy asked. She obviously had a certain order she liked to cover things in.

Morning and Afternoon Breaks

"Yes, and as a matter of fact, I'd like to do some very nice breaks. Not necessarily real expensive or elaborate, just different. You know, not your usual danish and coffee routine every day." You caught yourself sounding as though you knew what you were doing.

"Sure, we've been doing some great things with morning and afternoon breaks. I like to be creative. Let me get your times down first ..."

"Okay, we'll want a break each morning at 10:30 and again at 2:30 in the afternoon." You quickly shifted your meeting planners kit to the pages on menu selections for breaks. "Have coffee and orange juice each morning and what do you suggest instead of danish . . . maybe some doughnuts? I see on your ..."

"Hey, slow down a little, I'm trying to write all this down ya know!"

"Oops, sorry 'bout that."

"Okay, now we need something each morning to go with the coffee and orange juice." Apparently Wendy had caught up with you now. "How about doughnuts and muffins one morning, some sausage and ham biscuits the next morning, and pecan cinnamon rolls on Friday?" Wendy suggested.

"Ooh, that sounds yummy. I don't see the sausage and ham biscuits on the menu. How much would they be?" you asked. You remembered that you were to make sure you understood all prices.

"They are $1.50 each. We'd put in fifty, probably half ham, half sausage. It's a little more expensive than danish or doughnuts, but I think your attendees will really enjoy it."

You quickly calculated in your mind that the danish was approximately $1.00 each, so this was more expensive, but you loved the idea. The boss had given you some leeway on breaks and actually seemed quite pleased that you wanted to make them fun and interesting. The only restriction he had placed on "fun and interesting" was—NO BELLY DANCERS ! ! ! !

"Ms. Hawthorne? Did you hear what I said?"

"Oh, excuse me, and uh, please, call me Marty. I was just thinking of something the boss told me. Uh, yes, let's go with your suggestions on the breaks. How much coffee and orange juice do you think we'll need each day?"

"I figure on three gallons of coffee at the morning break and one and a half gallons of orange juice. You tell me if you want more orange juice. It has been my experience that not everyone will drink both. Our banquet houseman will check with your boss before replenishing any item. I suggest that you cut the coffee in half for the afternoon break and add some soft drinks."

Wendy had been asked this question a million times before and could figure quantities very quickly.

"Sounds good to me. Now, what do you recommend for the afternoon breaks? I mean, to go with the coffee and soft drinks. I'd like to make these a little different as well," you continued. "How about some fresh fruit cups or ice cream? Do you ever do any make-it-yourself ice cream sundaes?"

"That's a great idea, Marty! Uh, let's see ... We do offer ice cream at $1.50 per person. Let me check with the chef and get back to you on a price for all *follow-up*   the fixins'. I'll make a note of that right now. Probably shouldn't be more than additional $0.50 per person. That will be good for ... maybe Thursday. How about the fresh fruit cup on Wednesday and some granola bars and cookies on Friday? Granola bars . . . let's put 25 of those . . . they'll be $1.00 each and then how about two and a half dozen cookies at $3.00 a dozen?" Wendy was sure that sounded like a good mix: Something healthy and something not-so-healthy but delicious.

"Great, but you've got to slow down. I'm writing too you know." You had everything written but the granola bars and the cookies. "Okay, I have it. Sounds terrific. What's next?"

This was going much faster than you had expected. Fortunately, the telephone hadn't rung off the hook the way it usually does.

Blocking Sleeping Rooms

"We need to talk about any sleeping accommodations you need," said Wendy. "When you were here I believe you said you would need approximately thirty sleeping rooms. Is that right?"

"I have thirty attendees from out of town. I could need a few more or a few less than that. Single rooms, we don't want to double them up," you answered. You really needed guidance here. You were hoping that Wendy would pick up on this and advise you what to block.

"Why don't we block thirty-five rooms with a two

week cut-off. Uh, that will be July 23rd. Can you have the names for me by then?"

"I think so—I'll just tell the sales reps they have to let me know or they won't have a room." You weren't real sure you had the authority to be so demanding, but you knew a two week cut-off was customary. *follow-up*

"Well, we'll work with you if we can—right now let's shoot for thirty-five rooms. This way, we might have a few too many rooms reserved, but at least you are covered if you need them. Will they be arriving the night before—on August 6th?"

"Yes, and departing the morning of August 9th." You felt you had at least a working knowledge of room reservations. You had, on occasion, made reservations for Mr. Moreland.

"Do you want to guarantee them for late arrival?" Wendy asked.

Oh boy, you thought, what did *How to Plan and Book Meetings and Seminars* say that meant? This is the part where you could cost your company bundles of money if you goof.

Wendy came to your rescue.

"You do understand that if you guarantee them for late arrival and do not cancel them by 6 P.M., you will be charged for them? However, if you reserve them as 6 P.M.'s they will be let go at six. If you have later arrivals, they could lose their rooms. Do you have any idea when they will arrive?" Wendy's eyes shifted to the line on the booking entry that asked for arrival time.

"No, I have no idea. I guess we had better guarantee them for late arrival. I will notify my attendees that if they don't let me know they aren't coming, so that I can cancel them in time, we will charge them for the room." *follow-up*

"Did you want the rooms that overlooked the lake?" Wendy knew you had liked those rooms.

"No, we decided that the ones on the street side would be sufficient." The rooms on the lake had been magnificent, but you and your boss had decided that the attendees would not be in their rooms that much and the street side would suffice this time. After all, there was a $15.00 difference that, multiplied by thirty people for three nights amounted to a great deal of money.

"All right, that's thirty-five singles at $60.00 each, streetside, arriving August 6th, departing August 9th, guaranteed for late arrival, right?"

"That's it." you said. "But let me ask you something. What if I find out that our Vice President is coming in for a day or so? Could you get me one of those nice suites we looked at for something less than an arm and a leg?"

"I think that could be arranged. Tell you what. I'll make arrangements to "comp" it and throw in a wine and cheese basket if you pick up 30 rooms each night." Wendy offered.

"And if we don't pick up thirty rooms?" You knew there was going to be a catch here.

"I'll let you have one suite for half of the price. That would be $60.00. Okay?"

"Okay, I don't know if he will be coming, but if he does, I want him to have a nice room. Thanks." You replied.

Meals and Menus

"That will take care of the rooms, now let's talk about menus for the dinner and three lunches. Do you want the buffet dinner? It is truly a scrumptious spread." Wendy said enthusiastically.

"Yes, the buffet. We'd like the Baked Ham and the Chicken as our hot entrees."

"Okay . . . Now you know our hotel policy requires that you guarantee fifty persons for a buffet meal. Do you understand what that means?"

"It means that I must guarantee a minimum of fifty persons, and I pay for fifty even if I have thirty-five, right?"

"That's right. Our chef prepares for ten percent over your guarantee on all of your meals. So, we'll be prepared for fifty-five people. You know also, that we require a guarantee forty-eight hours prior to the food function. I think I told you that. I'll make a note here that you want the buffet dinner with ham and chicken. Have you had a chance to look over the lunch selections?"

"Yes, I have. Would you like to write them down?" you said with all honesty.

"I certainly would. You really have done some wonderful advance preparation. I can't believe we are going to book this entire three day meeting in one phone call. I wish all the secretaries who called me were this well prepared." Wendy said with all sincerity.

Wendy was truly delighted to find someone who had all the answers to all her questions. She had held so many hands, guided so many secretaries through the maze of meeting planning.

"Since we'll have three lunches, I'd like to have beef on Wednesday and Friday and chicken on Thursday. How about the Salad, London Broil, and Pecan Pie for dessert on Wednesday? I'll wait a minute for you to get that down. Ready? Okay, on Thursday, the Soup of the Day, Chicken Breast Parmesan, and Key Lime Pie. On Friday, Fresh Fruit Cup, Sirloin of Beef, Apple Pie. Let me know when you have that and I'll go on."

"All right I have it, is there anything else?"

"Yes, one of our district managers has a birthday on Thursday. Can we arrange for a birthday cake to be served at lunch time?"

"Certainly. I will order one from a nearby bakery that does some really nice cakes. I'll get back with you on the price for that. Just 'Happy Birthday'? Uh, what's his name?" Wendy asked.

follow-u

"Jerry Boyer," you replied.

"B as in Boy? o-y-e-r? Okay, no problem.

Bar Arrangements

"Now I need to ask you about the bar. You want cocktails from six o'clock until seven o'clock. Is that an open bar on a per drink basis or by the bottle?" You sounded so assured that Wendy assumed you knew the difference.

"We'd like to have an open bar on a per drink basis. Serve call brands. Let's see, those drinks will be $2.50 each, right?" You had gone over the liquor requirements very carefully with your boss.

"Yes, that's right. Would you also like beer and wine available?" Wendy knew they usually included it on the bars because so many people preferred it to hard liquor. Women in the group were especially appreciative of being able to get a glass of white wine.

"Yes, we would like regular and light beer as well as your house rose and chablis. Will we be charged on a per drink basis for that?" You were not real sure about the beer and wine prices. You remembered reading something about liters . . .

"Beer and wine are $1.75 each. All right, I have that . . . Beer—regular and light . . . Wine, uh, rose and chablis . . . available on the bar at $1.75 each. Those are all plus-plus you know: plus tax and tip."

"Yes, I understand. The gratuity is sixteen percent isn't it?" You had learned that by carefully reading the menus. Confirmation never hurt . . . "Oh, I almost forgot! What about a bartender charge? Is there one?"

"Our bartender charge is $40.00. That will apply only if you do not exceed $150.00 in liquor sales. That will be spelled out on the contract. I really don't think your group will have any trouble exceeding $150.00."

Both of you laughed. You because you've heard some real good stories about the way your group drinks at these meetings. Wendy laughed because she has seen groups half this size drink that much.

Hors d'Oeuvres

"May I suggest some hors d'oeuvres? Perhaps something light. Hmmm . . . how about cheese and crackers, fresh vegetables, and some canapes, nothing heavy. They are, after all, going to go right to the buffet table at seven o'clock. It's still a good idea to give them a little something to nibble on during the cocktail hour. How's that sound?" Wendy had put that together very quickly but it sounded good to you.

"Fine. I have the hors d'oeuvres sheet in front of me. How many of each of these do you think we'll need?" You knew they were priced by the trays of fifty pieces. Based on what you had read, you should order six pieces per person per hour. That would be three hundred pieces for fifty people. That would be six trays or the equivalent thereof. You too could think pretty fast on your feet.

"Well, let's have two trays of each. That should be enough to tide them over. That's eighty plus ninety plus seventy." You could hear Wendy's calculator again and knew she had realized you were interested in the cost of each area of your meeting. "The hors d'oeuvres will be $240.00 plus—"

"I know, plus-plus. Got it. How long did it take you to learn how to spell hors d'oeuvres?"

"A long time, believe me," Wendy admitted.

"I'm having a terrible time with it. There. Now, what's next?" You knew you had not discussed billing procedures. Maybe that was next.

Billing Information

"Now we need to talk about how you want to pay for certain things. I'll need to know how you want to take care of group charges, that's the group meals we just set up, the cocktail party, the group breaks, audio visual equipment, the birthday cake and the meeting room charge. ..."

"Oops, will there be a meeting room charge?" you interrupted. You had not expected there to be one, considering the amount of business you were booking. In fact, you would be very disappointed if there was a charge.

"The Washington room rents for $100.00 a day. I think I can get you a reduced rate on that . . . Uh," Wendy had a feeling there might be some resistance to a charge.

"How about getting it removed entirely? I don't think Mr. Moreland will pay a meeting room charge. Seems to me that this is a large piece of business and ..." You had read in the book that if you disagreed with something, tell your contact.

follow-up   "I'll see what I can do then about getting it removed. When I call you back on these few menu prices I'll let you know what I found out on the meeting room charge. Okay?" Wendy had already made up her mind that you weren't going to be charged for the room but did have to get approval from her boss in order to waive it.

"Okay, sounds good."

"Now what were you asking me? I'm sorry, I interrupted you ..."

"We were talking about group charges that the company will be responsible for." Wendy began again.

"Oh yes, can you bill us for those charges?"

"Sure, I'll send you a credit application today. You'll

need to list a couple other hotels where you have had prior billings, some other trade references, it's pretty standard stuff . . . nothing real complicated. You will need to get it back to me as soon as possible. We have to have it approved prior to the start of the meeting or you will have to pay on departure for everything ..." Wendy explained.

She always made this very clear to her clients. Then if they didn't do their part, she was under no obligation to them. No last minute exceptions.

"Okay, I understand ..." You knew from reading your book that this was standard operating procedure.

"Now, who will be paying for sleeping rooms, tax on those rooms, and incidentals? Do you know what incidentals are?" Wendy was being helpful.

"Yes, that's meals, snacks, uh, gift shop items, phone calls, laundry."

"Bar charges. Don't forget those."

"The individual attendees will pay for their incidentals. The company will pay for everything else."

"Okay, that's rooms, tax, and group charges to the master account to be direct billed pending credit approval. Individuals will be responsible for their own incidentals." It sounded as if the two of you were beginning to wrap things up. "We will require a credit card from each of the attendees, as they check in, to guarantee payment of their incidentals. If they don't have one, they won't be able to charge anything to their rooms."

"That's okay." you replied.

"That covers everything I need to get from you. I'll have these contracts typed right away and in the mail to you as soon as possible. You should have them in *follow-up* about three or four days. I'll try to get those prices for you this afternoon. If I can't set them before the contracts go out, I'll put "To Be Advised" in the proper places and call you when I get the numbers. Try to get your boss to sign them and send them back to me as *follow-up* soon as you can.

"We certainly are glad that you chose the Benton III and I assure you that everything will go very smoothly and our staff will do a good job for you. It is such a pleasure to work with someone who knows what they want and can effectively communicate those wishes. Remember, if you have any changes or questions, please don't hesitate to call me or my staff."

Wendy's words were very reassuring and you were looking forward to working with her. She was obviously a sincere and competent person and you felt very confident that she would do everything possible to see that your meeting went well.

"I'm sure I've forgotten some things," you said, although you could not imagine what. "I'll probably call you a million times."

"That's okay. That's what I'm here for. Have a good weekend. Bye now."

"Thanks for your help. Bye." As you hung up the telephone you glanced at the clock. It was almost five. "Well," you thought, "that's enough damage for one day. It's Friday and I'm ready to go home. That really wasn't so hard after all."

Chapter 15

Staying on Schedule

Well, what did you think? Sounded pretty easy huh? It is easy. Your conversation won't be exactly like this one, but that doesn't matter. This is only an example.

Completing the Booking

You might find, however, that you and your contact become engaged in small talk when you discover your kids attend the same school, or that each of you are having the same problems with your new computers. That won't get the meeting booked. Try to stay on target.

It is possible though that for one reason or another, you were unable to complete the booking in the initial conversation. Perhaps because the phones began ringing off the hook, yours or hers, or that very important client arrived early for your meeting! Whatever the reason, you may have to continue your conversation later in the day. At any rate, get the job done as soon as possible. Don't start the booking and finish it a week later. Be responsible in your timing. Remember too, it's a lot easier when you are prepared and minimize further calling back and forth between you and the hotel. If you go into this unprepared you'll cause yourself and the hotel a lot of grief; to say nothing of the time wasted in the process.

follow-up

When you returned to work on Monday you would begin to clean up your notes and sort out the follow-up that will keep you on schedule.

Marking the Calendar, Making Notes

Make a file folder marked "Meeting—Benton III Hotel August 7,8,9" (or, if you've already made one, continue to use it). Put everything pertaining to the meeting into that file: your menus, contract copies, all notes from the very beginning to the end. Document every conversation you have with the boss, the hotel, and the attendees and/or their secretaries. Future disputes can be kept to a minimum with these notes as backup.

Stay on track by using a large calendar to note all deadlines. Mark your deadlines, your attendees' deadlines and the hotel's deadlines.

I don't know what your lead time will be but, for discussion sake, let's say you have three weeks before the meeting. (And you thought I'd lost my sense of humor!)

Right away you'll want to pay particular attention to receipt of the contract, getting it signed by the boss, and getting it back to the hotel. If you promised to check with the boss and get back with your contact on any information, do that as quickly as possible so as not to hold up execution of the contract. Your letters to the attendees will also take top priority at this time.

If hotel deadlines approach and pass with no results, call your contact, I hope it will not be necessary, but you are even allowed to "bug", "badger", or "harass" if necessary to get them on the ball. You are the customer and it's your money, so you've got the right to ask as many questions and check back as often as you think necessary.

communicate

Verbal and Written Confirmations

It is particularly important for you to have a copy of everything you and your contact agree upon. Verbal confirmation may be valid but it is not a good business habit. If you have changes or additions, you can make notations right on the copy of the contract once you have it. You'll find a sample contract in the appendix as an example. Make sure you get the boss to look over the contract and sign it as soon as possible after receiving it. Return the proper copy to the hotel and keep one copy for yourself. I think you will find that the hotel will honor their deadlines and promises more readily if they see that you expect them to stay on schedule and do so yourself.

Letters to Attendees

Your letter to your attendees should go out right away. We have only touched briefly on its contents. In addition to the necessary information (What? Where? When?), they will want to know more.

Include in your letter a brief agenda. This will tell

your attendees if they should expect a long break-free meeting with lunch on their own (uh-oh—didn't make quotas . . .) or a meeting with frequent breaks and a group "company paid" lunch (hmm . . . sounds a little more friendly, must have shown a profit).

Include directions to the hotel. A small general map of the city would be helpful to those who are not familiar with it. You can draw something yourself and note key areas such as the airport, train/bus stations, the main office, downtown, and, of course, the location of the hotel where the meeting will be held. Show major highways into the city. Give approximate mileage between key points. This will better orient your attendees to your city.

For those not driving in, getting from an arrival point like the airport, train station, etc, always presents a problem. You can provide solutions to this dilemma in your letter. Be sure to inquire whether the hotel provides transportation to and from these key locations. If they do, you are in luck. If not, call various taxi companies and get an idea of how much the fare will be from the airport or train station to the hotel. If there are limousine services available, include this information. If your company will pay for a rental car, so stipulate in the letter. If, upon arrival, your attendees are to call your office for transportation to the hotel (as is done in many *communicate* companies) tell them in the letter. Be sure to advise them though, should they arrive after business hours, which alternate transportations you will pay for.

Now you must work the typing and mailing of these letters into your already very busy schedule. You will send them right away and mark your calendar for the follow-up phone work to contact those you have not heard from. Remember, you have a two week cut-off from the hotel. That means if it is three weeks before the meeting right now, you have to have confirmation from all attendees in one week! That means you have to notify them and hear back from them in one short week (maybe you'll get lucky and have a four to six week lead time! I know, fat chance . . . Okay, so let's get back to reality. When you have a short lead time, you might have to give your attendees advance notice by tele-phone. Sometimes this seems like an impossible task but it might be worth your while in the long run.

communicate

Tell them they will receive a letter in the mail in the next few days that will explain further, but you must know if they are coming and you have to know by July 20th. (The hotel will have the "fire to your feet" on this rooming list so you might as well pass it along early in the game.) I know your hotel cut-off is July 23rd. Give yourself a little leeway. Mark your calendar on July 21st to phone anyone you have not heard from.

follow-up

If your attendees are still wishy-washy about con-firming, impress on them that you cannot guarantee them a seat or sleeping room at the meeting. Let it go at that. Your obligation has been fulfilled. Document every conversation with them (or their secretaries — and be sure to get the name of the secretary!) and place these notes in your meeting file. Basically what I want to stress here is that you have communicated in a timely manner, given them cut-off dates that are reasonable, and followed-up in a professional manner. You are obligated now to the attendees who are coming and seeing that their meeting goes well. We'll deal with the inevitable last minute additions later on.

follow-up

It would be an excellent idea to make a response chart to keep track of all information going out to the attendees and information coming in to you from them. It will include their name and area or territory, address, telephone number (fill this in ahead of time), the date they were notified of the meeting (by phone and/or letter), a "yes" or "no" column for whether or not they are coming to the meeting, another for whether or not they will require a sleeping room and, if so, arrival and departure dates. Make a column for the date they respond to you and a "remarks" column for explanations.

Room Lists and Equipment Rentals

Approximately two weeks before the meeting, you will be attending to rooming lists, equipment rentals, and various secretarial duties to help the boss prepare for her presentation.

If at all possible, it would be a good idea for you and the boss to go to the hotel for lunch. She needs to see the meeting room, meet the hotel contact, and get a general feel for the surroundings. Encourage her to do this. If there is something she doesn't approve of in the layout of the meeting room, now is the time to find this out, not the morning of the meeting. Be sure to make an appointment with your contact so that the meeting room will be available for viewing. Hopefully it will be a time when it has been cleaned or better yet, cleaned and set in a style similar to the one which you have ordered.

A rooming list will be due at this time. You will find a sample form in the appendix of this book. Be sure to clearly define each attendee (names spelled correctly, please) and the type of accommodation they will require. Have all arrival and departure dates correct (to the best of your knowledge. You did ask them. Remember?) Keep your copy of this rooming list handy because I can guarantee that you will have *communicate* additions and deletions to it. Be sure that, when one of your attendees calls in a change, that you communicate this immediately to the hotel. Make a notation of the date that you notified the hotel, and who you spoke with. Always record who made the change or cancellation (attendee or his/her secretary).

If you have reserved twin sleeping accommodations because you plan to double up the attendees, it will be your responsibility and yours alone to do.

Do not expect the hotel to have anything to do with pairing the individuals.

Most will not even make a change to your rooming list without your permission. When you prepare this list of who is rooming with whom make sure you take two things into consideration: First, rank within the company and second, compatibility of attendees.

Sales representatives should not be paired with Vice Presidents. (Rank does have its privileges. Vice Presidents are rarely paired with anybody),

Keep similar rank paired.

Consider also the compatibility of your pairings. You should know that smokers prefer to room with smokers, drinkers with drinkers, married with married, singles with singles, night owls with night owls, and, of course, guys with guys and gals with gals, etc. (of these latter groups, any other arrangements must be made by the individuals). Compatibility also encompasses personalities. If you are aware of any controversy among your attendees, please try to keep peace on the rooming list, even if it comes down to giving two individuals single rooms to avoid World War III! It won't hurt to run your pairings by the boss to be sure he/she is in agreement.

Make compatible pairings.

If you haven't done so, now is the time to make any arrangements for equipment rental. If your boss will require projectors, sound systems, or any other audiovisual equipment for her meeting, you need to reserve it in your company name at this time. Give the rental company the dates you will need the equipment and discuss pick up and return dates as well. Be sure you understand the charges involved with these rentals. Make a note and include them in your file. Make a note also on your calendar for you or your boss to pick these items up. (Since charges are usually based on a twenty-four hour basis, plan your pick up and return based on economics as well as convenience.)

In addition to all of your usual duties as secretary/ administrative assistant you will undoubtedly become very involved with the boss' preparation for the meeting. She will have countless reports, graphs, charts, outlines, etc. for you to type or copy, re-type and re-copy. You should expect to be asked for help in this area. You should also expect a "Thank You[77].

You can be very valuable to your boss as the day of the meeting approaches. You can help her stay organized by giving her constant little reminders. Such as, "Did you get the numbers you needed from Tom?[77] or "I'll type that chart if you are finished with it" or "I called home office and got these projections you needed for your presentation. How are you coming on it?" You might also want to suggest that she practice her presentation in front of you.

Meal Guarantees

In the last few days before the meeting, you will be calling in meal guarantees (generally forty-eight to seventy-two hours prior to the function). Use your response sheet to determine your final numbers. Be sure to include local attendees and any special guests that may come just for a particular meal function. Order the number of meals you think you will need. You can't do any better than that. If one or two don't show up, you'll have to deal with that within your company policy. The hotel must be paid for the guaranteed amount or actual number, whichever is greater.

We discussed earlier that the hotel will prepare for a certain amount over the guarantee. Be sure you know

what that number is. If you think you will need fifty meals, you should order fifty. The hotel will prepare for fifty-five if they prepare for ten percent over. That should cover any last minute additions. Be sure to inform the contact if you should find out about additional attendees even as late as a couple of hours ahead of the meal.

Changes

Continue to communicate any and all changes,   *communicate* additions, or deletions to your contact as you learn of them. Don't store up changes for dumping at the last minute. Copies of your contract will be distributed to the hotel staff as early as ten days to two weeks prior to the function. All changes, additions, or deletions known up to that time should be on that contract. From the time of distribution until the meeting, your contact must submit any further changes, additions, or deletions to the staff separately and individually as amendments, memos, or change notices. Ever heard the phrase "I didn't get that additional memo?" You don't want that to be an excuse for a major disaster at your meeting. Always notify your contact of any changes as soon as possible.

Chapter 16

The Big Day

If you're not actually running the meeting your-self, your presence in the office on the day of the meeting is most valuable. Try not to be sick or even late on that day. It will be very reassuring to your boss to know that you are holding down the fort since he cannot be in two places at the same time.

Business As Usual

It may very well be that your duties today are to handle routine daily business and nothing related to the meeting. This could happen if you have done a thorough job of booking it. Every detail has been at-tended to and hopefully all goes smoothly.

There are, however, a couple of things that could

still come up. While your boss is physically in the meeting the hotel contact will still need to rely on your judgement if something arises that needs immediate attention. She certainly will not interrupt him.

Last Minute Changes

You might need to make a decision regarding the Big Boss' sleeping room (since he has decided, at the last possible minute, to come to the meeting). He will be arriving some time this afternoon and there is no suite available. You will need to make a determination on the type of accommodation to reserve for him.

The florist wants to substitute mums for daisies in the centerpieces for dinner on Wednesday night. They have to know today. You will also make that decision.

It is hard to say what might come up, but you will need to take care of whatever does. Perhaps the boss has said that he will call you at lunch time to pick up his messages. If so, you might be able to ask his opinion on some things you are just not sure of and call the hotel back immediately with your answer.

The Worst That Can Happen

I don't want to alarm you, but there are also some things that can happen that will disrupt your boss' meeting no matter how carefully it has been booked.

These are unavoidable, often unforeseeable, events that must be dealt with if and when they occur. After you read this, just tell the boss jokingly that if anything unavoidable happens like a flood or a fire, to call you and you'll give him some suggestions.

The range of these occurrences might be anything from catastrophic to seemingly minor:

* Flooded meeting room due to bursting of water pipes or leaking ceilings
* Fire (or just fire alarms)
* Long power outages (no windows in the meeting room and no where to move to)
* Breakdown in heating/air conditioning systems (no portable heaters or electric fans.)
* An absent or extremely late instructor/speaker
* Meeting/Banquet room not set up (it is time to begin)
* Hotel runs out of food on the buffet line
* Missing audio-visual equipment
* Last minute room assignment changes
* Cancellations/No shows (Class has twenty-five attendees instead of fifty)
* Additions (to an already "full" hotel)
* Late coffee breaks

These are some of the disasters and mini-disasters that can occur. As you can see, some of these are unavoidable, but some are due to human error and negligence.

How you will deal with events such as these will depend on whether your group is a "tough-it-out" or "cut-and run" type and the degree of the disaster. The most important thing to remember is to stay calm. The hotel will work with you on alternate arrangements. Chances are that they are just as upset about the problem as your boss is.

Catastrophic Events

In the case of extreme incapacitation of a meeting room (fire, flood, prolonged power outage) with no alternate meeting room to move to, you might try to move your meeting to a nearby hotel. You might have

to cancel the meeting for that day, extend everyone's length of stay, and begin the next day at a new location. Discuss the possibilities of the current hotel providing transportation for your attendees to and from the new location. This might be in exchange for leaving your sleeping accommodations booked there. (They will retain the revenue and your attendees will not be inconvenienced by having to pack and move.)

Your boss might want to discuss the alternatives with the attendees. In the case of a fire, they might not feel safe staying in that hotel. In the case of a prolonged power outage, the power may also be off in the sleeping rooms so they could not stay there. There will be numerous avenues of approach if you will all stay calm and level headed. There will be a lot of room for compromise and negotiation in situations like this.

Intermediate Disturbances

In the area of intermediate disturbances (heating/ air conditioning breakdowns, absent instructor, room not set up, running out of food on the buffet line, missing equipment), I would suggest again that the situation be weighed and carefully thought through.

If you have a "tough-it-out" group of people in your meeting, they might be able to add or subtract clothing to get through the heating or air conditioning problem. Of course, there are limits to how far this can go, especially in a co-ed group. Ask for fans or portable heaters. Again, depending on the weather, you might have to move the meeting to another location altogether.

An absent or extremely late instructor can be a real embarrassment indeed. I suggest that your boss have a back-up plan. He might decide to go on without the speaker and give an alternate presentation himself.

Chances are good that if he prepares a back-up presentation he won't wind up needing one.

If the meeting room is not set up on time your boss has a right to be extremely angry. However, it won't do anyone any good if he makes a scene. He should remain calm and get in touch with his contact immediately. He should receive quick, on-the-spot attention and an accurate estimate of how much time it will take to prepare the room. He should then inform his attendees accordingly and ask them to leave the area so the work can be done more quickly and report back in a given time (then he can get out the tar and feathers!). I do strongly suggest that your boss arrive at the hotel and check that meeting room at least an hour ahead of the start time.

During a buffet meal, there should be frequent checks by the hotel staff of the level of remaining food. To be on the safe side, your boss should keep a watchful eye on it. At the first sign of running low he should inform a server or even the chef himself.

Missing audio-visual equipment can be a cause for alarm. Depending on how much of it is missing, and whether it is being furnished by the hotel or from an outside source, it might be possible to rearrange parts of the presentation and proceed without much delay. If all of it is missing, again, your boss might need to delay the start of the meeting altogether until it arrives.

More Minor Problems

Some of the more minor disturbances (last minute room assignment changes, cancellations, additions, late coffee breaks) are easier to deal with.

Last minute room assignment changes may delay the start of the meeting only a few minutes. You might have informed your attendees in your letter that they would be meeting in the Washington Room and, for some reason, it has been changed to the Madison Room. The hotel will usually have a reader board somewhere in the lobby. This is a posting of the daily meetings and banquets and where each will take place. The change in your meeting room should appear on this board. It would also be a good idea for a note to be placed on the door or wall of the Washington Room directing your attendees to the Madison Room. Note: This should not be standard practice and the hotel had better have a good reason for changing the room.

Cancellations are a fact of life. A drastic reduction in your estimate, say as much as 50%, rarely happens but is still a possibility. This may be due to inclement weather or transportation problems. If this happens, I suggest that your boss speak with the hotel contact, perhaps the general or assistant manager in this case, and discuss the problem. You might be able to come to an agreeable compromise on meal and sleeping room guarantees.

If you find that you need additional sleeping rooms and the hotel is full, you can do one of two things. You might try to double up some of your attendees if they are singles in a twin room with an extra bed, or you might have to make arrangements at another nearby hotel. These attendees can then be transported to and from the meeting hotel each day. Be sure your contact informs the kitchen of any additional meals required and the set-up personnel of any additional seating.

Late coffee breaks really get my dander up! There is little or no excuse for this happening. And yet, I'll bet there isn't a hotel in the world that it doesn't happen to on occasion. This is a real aggravation to most bosses. Late breaks can be very distracting. Your boss will be trying to give his presentation and if there is no sign of the coffee break and it's time for it, he'll also be wondering if the hotel has forgotten about it or if it is on its way .... His attendees are getting restless . . . What to do . . . ?

It is however, an avoidable problem. Make sure that you impress on the hotel contact that those breaks cannot be late. Tell them it is a real sore spot with your boss. Hotels have got to wage war on the late coffee break. (At the hotel where I worked, late coffee breaks were not tolerated and our housemen knew it.)

Well, these are just some of the problems that can arise. I'm sure that sooner or later you will be able to add to this list. These are, thank goodness, exceptions to the rule. Some of it is, as I said, human error (we are all human). Some of it is not. I would hope that you and your boss will look objectively at any problems that may occur and consider why it happened. Then make your decision whether to continue using that hotel.

Let's hope that everything goes as planned and the worst thing that happens is that the houseman has to run for an extra extension cord or three or four more coffee cups.

You should have a problem-free meeting.

Basically, you have no real control over these things at this point. What you do have control over is the smooth operation of your business while the boss is away. Concentrate on handling as much of the daily business as you can and take a lot of good phone messages.

Chapter 17

Success Summary

I am basically an optimist. I believe that your first booking will go so well that I have called this chapter the Success Summary. It's time for kudos, rewards, and pats on the back. We won't spend much time on reprimands. We are, after all, only learning to crawl . . . We'll walk, and even run, in due time.

Rewards and Reprimands

It is important for you to schedule some time with the boss after the meeting (before you go on vacation) to discuss, in detail, how you could improve your next booking.

Try to be objective in your discussion. No matter how well it went, there is always room for improvement. Ask specific questions. Be ready for constructive criticism. Take notes. Do not take too much of the boss' time but do not settle for an answer like "Everything went all right."

If a client said that to me at the hotel, I immediately knew something had gone wrong that I wasn't aware of. It was a signal of a silent complaint. Maybe something which the client felt went wrong at all hotels, something he felt wasn't worth mentioning. Who knows, at any rate, I persisted and usually found the cause of their concern. After looking into a problem, no matter how minor, and assuring them that it would not go uncorrected they were usually genuinely pleased.

You will work very hard on that first booking. I hope you will take great pride in trying to make it perfect. You cannot continue to improve unless you know exactly what went on. If the coffee breaks were late— You need to know that. If the sleeping rooms were too hot—You need to know that. If the check out procedure got bogged down and someone missed their plane because of it—You need to know. You need to know because you are going to inform the hotel contact of your displeasure in these areas. If you don't scream bloody murder when these things happen, they will happen again.

By the same token, if you forgot to order a special meal for one of the attendees, you should take the blame. If you told the boss that you would take care of Mr. Boyer's birthday cake and you didn't, you let him down. If you pulled your estimate from thin air and didn't discuss it with the boss and the hotel ended up moving the meeting to a different location at the last minute, causing the meeting to start late, again, you did it! It isn't easy to get everything just right. It takes time and it takes practice. Your knowledge will increase with every booking.

Okay, enough of that. Now let's talk about what everyone did right! Once you get the sordid details from the boss about everything you and the hotel did wrong, you had better hear some praises about the things you did right! Drag them out of him if you have it.

It's important that you are left with a good feeling (warm fuzzies) about what you have just accomplished!

Lessons You Learned

Evaluate everything you learned by this experience. I'm sure the good things will far outweigh the bad. Ask yourself if the boss was happy with the arrangements. Notice I said "the arrangements". The boss' attitude will be influenced somewhat by how well the actual meeting went. Be careful that your booking doesn't take a beating because the mood of the meeting was not good. Also, if the mood of the meeting was positive, don't let your boss overlook the downside of any aspect of your booking. This conversation with the boss may reveal areas where he needs to be more specific in conveying his wishes to you. Good. Point this out to him if he did not make something clear to you in the beginning. This should be a learning experience for both of you.

Many companies have devised an all encompassing critique for the attendees to fill out. They are asked to evaluate the instructor's presentation, the hotel's facilities and services, and the overall accomplishments of the meeting. They may or may not include their name. You can then compile the results of these critiques to have an even better picture of the meeting in its entirety.

Evaluation of Performance

You should evaluate the hotel's performance in great detail. If you felt that they could have done a better job in certain areas, be sure to bring this to the attention of the contact. The unwritten bottom line to the hotel is this:

"Shape up or we'll ship out!"

The hotel business is highly competitive. They should be very concerned with keeping your business. If they are not, move on to someone who is. They are, after all, in the service industry and you should expect no less than the best.

Be sure, however, in your evaluation that you also take into consideration what you told the hotel. Do not blame them for insufficient information on your part.

If the hotel followed your instructions to the letter, then that's what you should send to them: a "Happy Letter".

Encourage your boss to send a letter to the hotel (to the attention of the General Manager) expressing his pleasure with the performance of the hotel staff at your recent meeting held there. Have him mention specific names of those individuals who went out of their way to insure the success of his meeting. You have no way of knowing how much this will mean to them.

Well, that about covers it. I hope that in some small way I have given you something to keep. Something that will make your life easier, whether it's the solid facts, suggestions, or just plain opinions that help you communicate better with the boss and the hotel contact. That's what this book is all about . . . Keep it handy, refer to it often and Good Luck!

Appendix

Site Inspection Report Form

SITE INSPECTION REPORT

HOTEL:_____   DATE OF VISIT:_____

ADDRESS: _____   TELEPHONE:_____

             _____

CONTACT: _____

Lobby
  Reception Area   _____

                _____

                _____

Meeting Room   _____

                _____

Restaurant   _____

                _____

Sleeping Rooms   _____

                _____

Grounds/Pool   _____

                _____

Staff   _____

                _____

                _____

Contract

BENTON III HOTEL
1000 ORCHARD LANE
JACKSONVILLE, FLA. 32207
(904) 763-1000

DAY AND DATE (Use separate sheet for each day)		MEETING TIMES:	MEAL TIMES: (Start - Finish)	
WEDNESDAY, AUGUST 7, 1986		9 AM 5 PM	BREAKFAST	N/A
COMPANY / ORGANIZATION			LUNCH	12:00 - 1:00 PM
TOYS INTERNATIONAL			DINNER	7:00 - 9:00 PM
ADDRESS (Include Street Name, Number, City, State, Zip Code)			*OTHER	6:00 - 7:00 PM
3388 UNICORN LANE JACKSONVILLE, FLA 32210			(COCKTAILS)	

CONTACT (S)		PHONE NUMBER		
Ms. HAWTHORNE / Mr. MORELAND		782-0018	[X] BUSINESS	[ ] RESIDENCE

ATTENDANCE	DEPOSIT (Date & Amount)	MARQUEE/LOBBY READER BOARD INSTRUCTIONS	MEETING ROOM CHG
50	N/A	TOYS INTERNATIONAL	NONE

SEATING SPECIFICATIONS (Meeting and Meals) / MENUS (Except Breaks)

TIME	LOCATION	TIME	LOCATION
9:00 AM	WASHINGTON ROOM	12:00	JEFFERSON ROOM
CLASSROOM FOR 50		TOSSED SALAD	
NOTE PADS AND PENCILS		LONDON BROIL, SLICED	
WATER, GLASSES		APPROPRIATE VEGETABLE/POTATO	
ASHTRAYS AND MATCHES		ASSORTED LUNCHEON ROLLS, BUTTER	
OVERHEAD PROJECTOR @ $35.00 + TAX		PECAN PIE	
		COFFEE, TEA	
			$8.75 ++
12:00	JEFFERSON ROOM		
ROUNDS FOR 50	(BACK-UP FOR DINNER ALSO)	6:00 - 7:00	POOLSIDE
		(2) TRAYS CHEESE/CRACKERS @ $40.00 ++ EA	
		(2) TRAYS FANCY CANAPES @ $45.00 ++ EA	
6:00	POOLSIDE	(2) TRAYS FRESH VEGETABLES @ $35.00 ++ EA	
ROUNDS FOR 50		7:00 - 9:00	POOLSIDE (JEFFERSON)
BUFFET TABLES		"BUFFET DINNER"	
PORTABLE BARS (2)		FRESH BAKED HAM, FRIED CHICKEN	
HORS D'OEUVRES TABLE (1)		(HOT ENTREES)	
TIKI TORCHES		ASSORTED FRESH VEGETABLES/POTATOES	
		VARIETY OF PIES, CAKES	
		BREADS, ROLLS, CROISSANTS	
		COFFEE, TEA	
			$15.95 ++

BREAKS / BAR

TIME	LOCATION	TIME	LOCATION
10:30	WASHINGTON ROOM	6:00 - 7:00	POOLSIDE (JEFFERSON)
(3) GALLONS COFFEE @ $14.00 GAL		X OPEN ____ CASH X PER DRINK ____ BOTTLE	
(1 1/2) GALLONS ORANGE JUICE @ $18.00 GAL			
(50) ASSORTED DOUGHNUTS/MUFFINS @1.00 EA		[ ] HOUSE@_____ [X] CALL@ 2.50 [ ] PREM@_____	
		[X] BEER@ 1.75 [X] WINE@ 1.75 [ ] OTHER@_____	
2:30		SPECIFY BRANDS AND AMTS IF APPLICABLE	
(1 1/2) GALLONS COFFEE @ $14.00 GAL		REG/LIGHT BEER; HOUSE WINES.	
(25) ASSORTED SOFT DRINKS @ $.60 EA			
(50) FRESH FRUIT CUPS @ $1.50 EA		ALL PRICES ARE PLUS TAX AND TIP	
		BARTENDER REQUIRED X YES ____ NO	
ALL PRICES ARE PLUS TAX AND TIP		CHARGE $40.00 APPLIES TO BAR WITH REVENUE LESS THAN $150.00	

SLEEPING ACCOMODATIONS / BILLING INFORMATION

35 SINGLS	@ 50.00 EA	ARRIVAL: 8/6/86
___ DBLS	@ EA	DEPARTURE: 8/9/86
___ TWNS	@ EA	
1 STES	@ 50.00 EA	CUT-OFF DATE: 7/23/86
*WINE/CHEESE - VICE PRESIDENT		

DETAILED BOOKING ENTRY ATTACHED- COPY TO HOTEL RESERVATIONIST.

X GTD
X CO.
___ C/C (See Booking Ent)
___ 5 PM'S

BILLING INFORMATION

___ ON DEPARTURE: ____ CHECK ____ C/C ____ CASH

X DIRECT BILL: CREDIT APPROVAL
___ Complete X Pending 7/9/86

CHARGES:	MASTER	INDIVIDUAL
Rooms	X	
Tax	X	
Incidentals		X
Group Charges	X	

ACCEPTED_____ DATE_____

Contract

BENTON III HOTEL
1000 ORCHARD LANE
JACKSONVILLE, FLA. 32207
(904) 763-1000

DAY AND DATE (Use separate sheet for each day)		MEETING TIMES:	MEAL TIMES: (Start - Finish)	
FRIDAY, AUGUST 8, 1986		9 AM 5 PM	BREAKFAST	ON OWN
COMPANY / ORGANIZATION			LUNCH	12:00 - 1:00 PM
TOYS INTERNATIONAL			DINNER	ON OWN
ADDRESS (Include Street Name, Number, City, State, Zip Code)			OTHER	
3388 UNICORN LANE JACKSONVILLE, FLA 32210				

CONTACT (S)		PHONE NUMBER		
Ms. HAWTHORNE / Mr. MORELAND		782-0018 [X] BUSINESS [ ] RESIDENCE		

ATTENDANCE	DEPOSIT (Date & Amount)	MARQUEE/LOBBY READER BOARD INSTRUCTIONS	MEETING ROOM CHG
50	N/A	TOYS INTERNATIONAL	NONE

SEATING SPECIFICATIONS (Meeting and Meals)

TIME	LOCATION
9:00 AM	WASHINGTON ROOM

CLASSROOM FOR 50
NOTE PADS AND PENCILS
WATER, GLASSES
ASHTRAYS AND MATCHES
OVERHEAD PROJECTOR @ $35.00 + TAX
CAROUSEL SLIDE PROJECTOR @ $35.00 + TAX

TIME	LOCATION
12:00	JEFFERSON ROOM

ROUNDS FOR 50

MENUS (Except Breaks)

TIME	LOCATION
12:00	JEFFERSON ROOM

FRESH FRUIT CUP
SIRLOIN OF BEEF, NOODLES
APPROPRIATE VEGETABLE
ASSORTED LUNCHEON ROLLS, BUTTER
APPLE PIE
COFFEE, TEA

$9.25 ++

BREAKS

TIME	LOCATION
10:30	WASHINGTON ROOM

(3)   GALLONS COFFEE @ $14.00 GAL
(1 1/2) GALLONS ORANGE JUICE @ $18.00 GAL
(50)   PECAN CINNAMON ROLLS @1.00 EA

2:30

(1 1/2) GALLONS COFFEE @ $14.00 GAL
(25)   ASSORTED SOFT DRINKS @ $.80 EA
        (INCLUDE DIET)
(25)   GRANOLA BARS @ $1.00 EA
(2 1/2) DOZ. COOKIES @ $3.50 DOZ

ALL PRICES ARE PLUS TAX AND TIP

BAR

TIME	LOCATION

____OPEN _____CASH _____PER DRINK _____BOTTLE

[ ] HOUSE@_____   [ ] CALL@_____   [ ] PREM@_____

[ ] BEER@_____   [ ] WINE@_____   [ ] OTHER@_____

SPECIFY BRANDS AND AMTS IF APPLICABLE

BARTENDER REQUIRED ____YES ____NO
CHARGE   APPLIES TO BAR WITH
REVENUE LESS THAN _____.

SLEEPING ACCOMODATIONS

35	SINGLS	@ 60.00	EA	ARRIVAL: 8/6/86
	DBLS	@	EA	DEPARTURE: 8/9/86
	TWNS	@	EA	
1	STES	@ *60.00	EA	CUT-OFF DATE: 7/23/86

*WINE/CHEESE - VICE PRESIDENT

DETAILED BOOKING ENTRY
ATTACHED- COPY TO HOTEL
RESERVATIONIST.

X GTD
X CO.
__ C/C (See Booking Ent)
__ 6 PM'S

BILLING INFORMATION

_ON DEPARTURE: ____CHECK ____C/C ____CASH

X DIRECT BILL: CREDIT APPROVAL
                    __Complete X Pending 7/9/86

CHARGES:	MASTER	INDIVIDUAL
Rooms	X	
Tax	X	
Incidentals		X
Group Charges	X	

ACCEPTED_____   DATE_____

Contract

BENTON III HOTEL
1000 ORCHARD LANE
JACKSONVILLE, FLA. 32207
(904) 763-1000

DAY AND DATE (Use separate sheet for each day)	MEETING TIMES:	MEAL TIMES: (Start - Finish)	
THURSDAY, AUGUST 8, 1986	9 AM 5 PM	BREAKFAST	ON OWN
COMPANY / ORGANIZATION		LUNCH	12:00 - 1:00 PM
TOYS INTERNATIONAL		DINNER	ON OWN
ADDRESS (Include Street Name, Number, City, State, Zip Code)		OTHER	
3388 UNICORN LANE JACKSONVILLE, FLA 32210			

CONTACT (S)	PHONE NUMBER		
Ms. HAWTHORNE / Mr. MORELAND	782-0018	[X] BUSINESS	[ ] RESIDENCE

ATTENDANCE	DEPOSIT (Date & Amount)	MARQUEE/LOBBY READER BOARD INSTRUCTIONS	MEETING ROOM CHG
50	N/A	TOYS INTERNATIONAL	NONE

SEATING SPECIFICATIONS (Meeting and Meals)

TIME	LOCATION
9:00 AM	WASHINGTON ROOM

CLASSROOM FOR 50
NOTE PADS AND PENCILS
WATER, GLASSES
ASHTRAYS AND MATCHES
OVERHEAD PROJECTOR @ $35.00 + TAX
CAROUSEL SLIDE PROJECTOR @ $35.00 + TAX

TIME	LOCATION
12:00	JEFFERSON ROOM

ROUNDS FOR 50

MENUS (Except Breaks)

TIME	LOCATION
12:00	JEFFERSON ROOM

SOUP DU JOUR
CHICKEN BREAST, PARMESAN
APPROPRIATE VEGETABLE/POTATO
ASSORTED LUNCHEON ROLLS, BUTTER
KEY LIME PIE
COFFEE, TEA

$8.50 ++

*** BIRTHDAY CAKE ***
"HAPPY BIRTHDAY - JERRY BOYER"

$50.00 ++

BREAKS

TIME	LOCATION
10:30	WASHINGTON ROOM

(3)   GALLONS COFFEE @ $14.00 GAL
(1 1/2) GALLONS ORANGE JUICE @ $18.00 GAL
(50)   ASSORTED SAUSAGE/HAM BISCUITS @$1.50 EA

2:30

(1 1/2) GALLONS COFFEE @ $14.00 GAL
(25)   ASSORTED SOFT DRINKS @ $.80 EA
         (INCLUDE DIET)
(50)   ICE CREAM CUPS WITH "FIXIN'S" @ $2.00 EA

ALL PRICES ARE PLUS TAX AND TIP

BAR

TIME	LOCATION

_____OPEN _____CASH _____PER DRINK _____BOTTLE

[ ] HOUSE@_____   [ ] CALL@_____ [ ] PREM@_____

[ ] BEER@_____   [ ] WINE@_____ [ ] OTHER@_____

SPECIFY BRANDS AND AMTS IF APPLICABLE

BARTENDER REQUIRED ____YES ____NO
CHARGE APPLIES TO BAR WITH
REVENUE LESS THAN_____

SLEEPING ACCOMODATIONS

35	SINGLS	@ 60.00	EA	ARRIVAL: 8/6/86
	DBLS	@	EA	DEPARTURE: 8/9/86
	TWNS	@	EA	
1	STES	@ 60.00	EA	CUT-OFF DATE: 7/23/86
	*WINE/CHEESE - VICE PRESIDENT			

DETAILED BOOKING ENTRY
ATTACHED- COPY TO HOTEL
RESERVATIONIST.

X GTD
X CO.
C/C(See Booking Ent)
5 PM'S

BILLING INFORMATION

_ON DEPARTURE: ___CHECK ___C/C ___CASH

X DIRECT BILL: CREDIT APPROVAL
                    ___Complete X Pending 7/9/86

CHARGES:	MASTER	INDIVIDUAL
Rooms	X	
Tax	X	
Incidentals		X
Group Charges	X	

ACCEPTED_____ DATE_____

Booking Entry/Room Reservations

BOOKING ENTRY	[X] DEFINITIVE [ ] TENTATIVE	BOOKED BY: Wendy Davis DATE BOOKED: 7/9/86

RATES		TOTAL ROOM NIGHTS
SINGLE	60.00	108
DOUBLE		
TRIPLE		ESTIMATED TOTAL VALUE
QUAD		6300.
COTS		
SUITES	*60.00	TRAVEL AGENT ___YES X NO
		COMMISSION %

GROUP NAME: TOYS INTERNATIONAL
CONTACT: MRS. HAWTHORNE
ADDRESS: 3388 UNICORN LANE
CITY, STATE, ZIP CODE: JACKSONVILLE, FL 32207
TELEPHONE NO. (AREA CODE): 782-0018 (904)

BENTON III

RESERVATIONS BY:

X ROOMING LIST   ___INDIVIDUAL   ___HOUSING BUREAU
___RESERVATION CARDS   ___THEIR FORMS   ___OTHER

DEPOSIT REQUIREMENTS: N/A

COMPLIMENTARY ROOMS
(1) WITH P/U OF 30
*otherwise 60.00
RESERVATION CUT-OFF
7/23/86

DAY —	FRI	SAT	SUN	MON	TUE	WED	THU	FRI	SAT	SUN	MON	TUE	WED	THU	FRI	
DATE —					8/6	8/7	8/8									
SINGLE						35	35	35								
DOUBLES																
TWINS																
SUITES						1	1	1								
OTHER																
TOTAL																

BILLING:	MASTER	INDIVIDUAL
ROOMS	X	
TAX	X	
INCIDENTALS		X
GROUP	X	

ARRIVAL:
___GROUP
X INDIVIDUAL

X GUARANTEED LATE
___X COMPANY
___CREDIT CARD
___6 PM'S

Room List Form

<u>GROUP ROOMING LIST</u>

Arrival:_____

Departure:_____

_____
(COMPANY NAME)

BENTON III

	NAME	ARRIVAL	DEPARTURE	ROOM TYPE
1.				
2.				
3.				
4.				
5.				
6.				
7.				
8.				
9.				
10.				
11.				
12.				
13.				
14.				
15.				
16.				
17.				
18.				
19.				
20.				

<u>ROOM TYPES:</u>

___A___ SINGLE (1 PERSON/1 BED)   ___C___ TWIN (2 PERSONS/2 BEDS)

___B___ DOUBLE (2 PERSONS/1 BED)   ___D___ SUITE (SPECIFY # PERSONS)

INDEX

LaVergne, TN USA
07 March 2011
219085LV00004B/31/P